Showcase 500
art necklaces

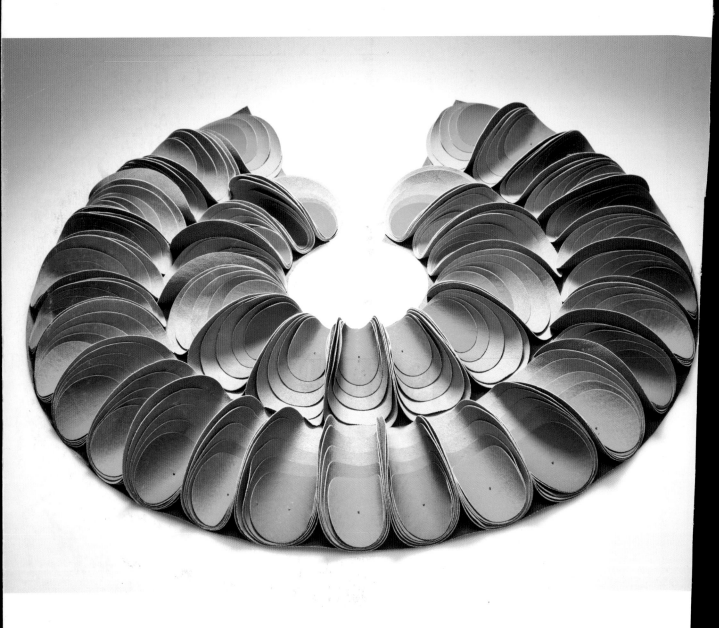

Showcase 500
art necklaces

Chunghi Choo, Juror

LARK JEWELRY
& BEADING

LARK JEWELRY & BEADING

An Imprint of Sterling Publishing
387 Park Avenue South
New York, NY 10016

SENIOR EDITOR
Ray Hemachandra

PRODUCTION EDITOR
Julie Hale

ART DIRECTOR
AND COVER DESIGNER
Matt Shay

FRONT COVER AND SPINE
Megan N. Clark
Stingray Feather Necklace,
2012

BACK COVER
clockwise from top left
Klaus Spies
Aquamarine Necklace, 2012

Kristin D. Levier
Sprig Necklace, 2012

Edgar A. Lopez
Caribbean Dream, 2012

Liaung Chung Yen
Secret Garden Necklace,
2012

Ashley Gilreath
I Am Who They Were, 2011

Misun Won
*Jogakbo Wrapping
Necklace*, 2011

FRONT FLAP
Tom Munsteiner
Aquamarine Necklace, 2012

BACK FLAP
Andrea Arias
Paseando por el Barrio, 2011

TITLE PAGE
**Marian Acosta
Contreras**
Fusion Neckpiece, 2010

OPPOSITE
Tia Kramer
*Necklace from the
Fluttering Series*, 2011

PAGE 6
Kathleen M. Carricaburu
Tree of Knowledge, 2011

ISBN 978-1-4547-0352-5

Library of Congress Cataloging-in-Publication Data

Hemachandra, Ray.
  Showcase 500 necklaces / Ray Hemachandra and Chunghi Choo.
    pages cm
  ISBN 978-1-4547-0352-5
  1. Necklaces. 2. Jewelry making. I. Choo, Chunghi. II. Title. III. Title: Showcase five hundred necklaces.
  NK7423.3.H46 2013
  745.594'2--dc23

2012041633

Distributed in Canada by Sterling Publishing
c/o Canadian Manda Group, 165 Dufferin Street
Toronto, Ontario, Canada M6K 3H6
Distributed in the United Kingdom by GMC Distribution Services
Castle Place, 166 High Street, Lewes, East Sussex, England BN7 1XU
Distributed in Australia by Capricorn Link (Australia) Pty. Ltd.
P.O. Box 704, Windsor, NSW 2756, Australia

For information about custom editions, special sales, and premium and corporate purchases, please contact Sterling Special Sales at 800-805-5489 or specialsales@sterlingpublishing.com.

Email academic@larkbooks.com for information about desk and examination copies. The complete policy can be found at larkcrafts.com.

Every effort has been made to ensure that all the information in this book is accurate. However, due to differing conditions, tools, and individual skills, the publisher cannot be responsible for any injuries, losses, and other damages that may result from the use of the information in this book.

Printed in Canada

2 4 6 8 10 9 7 5 3 1

contents

6 Introduction by Chunghi Choo

8 The Necklaces

416 Contributing Artists

420 About the Juror

420 Acknowledgments

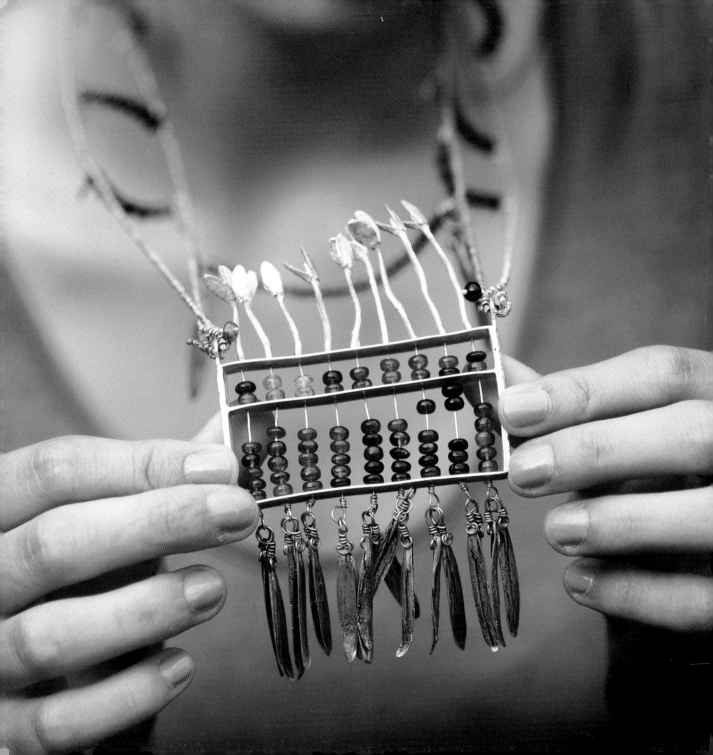

introduction

I want to congratulate all the artists who produced the creative neckpieces that appear in *Showcase 500 Art Necklaces*. I hope that the publication of this book helps promote awareness of outstanding creative contemporary craft generally and art jewelry specifically.

Being a practitioner in many mediums of contemporary craft and a teacher of jewelry, metal arts, and mixed media for half a century, and also being an extensive traveler, I have seen countless ancient and modern body ornaments in museums, museum storage rooms, art schools, galleries, and the design and fashion industries. I was delighted that approximately 3,000 contemporary art necklaces, many of which are just as awe-inspiring as those I've seen around the world, were submitted for consideration in this publication.

You will likely notice that many of the necklaces I have included show extensive mixed media work or complex beading work. In both North America and internationally, the trends in making art objects such as creative neckpieces are now wide open to the free use of varied materials, found objects, and flexible mediums. The necklaces are made with nearly countless techniques, including traditional, contemporary, and innovative cutting-edge technologies.

Artists typically explore new materials and techniques in order to produce fresh-looking jewelry. Many of these pieces are colorful, some are whimsical, and still others are quite subtle in their creative use of different materials and techniques. Modern technologies help speed up artists' creative production processes and expand their technical possibilities, but of course this new, ever-evolving frontier of jewelry-making is no guarantee of good-quality designs. If an artist does not have a strong, clear design sensibility, these industrial technologies will be of little use. I hope you feel that many of the pieces represented in this book strike the balance well and correctly.

I see many people wearing innumerable styles of earrings today, but art necklaces still have not achieved the same level of commonality. Artistic neckpieces can be integrated successfully with one's personality, clothing, and tastes to enhance a person's general sense of fashion. But of course people can only learn this lesson through the wearing of art necklaces, not through art lectures or book introductions. People must own pieces to be engaged with them and enjoy wearing them. In so doing, they come to appreciate this type of ornament more as both artwork and fashion.

Whether you wear art necklaces yourself or are simply a fan or jeweler-practitioner of the form, I trust this volume will enrich your appreciation of art necklaces and body ornament more generally. It was an honor and thrill to be selected and to serve as the juror of this book, and I truly hope you enjoy it.

Chunghi Choo
F. Wendell Miller Distinguished Professor of Art,
University of Iowa
Distinguished Member of the Society
of North American Goldsmiths
Elected Fellow of the American Craft Council

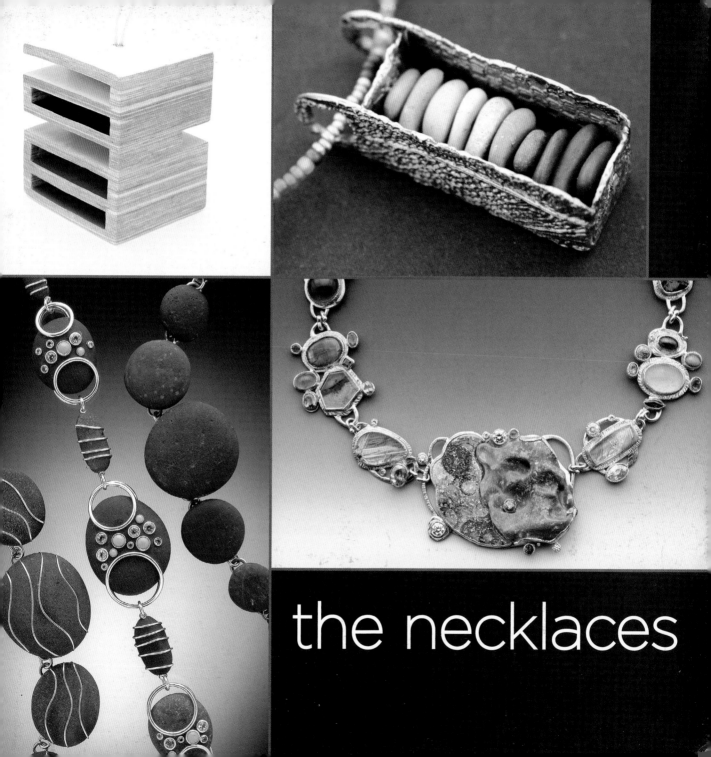

the necklaces

DAVID GIULIETTI
Pierced Chalcedony Necklace ■ 2011
Pendant: 5 x 4 x 1 cm
Sterling silver, 18-karat gold, chalcedony,
sapphire; oxidized, forged, fabricated,
pierced, hand engraved, cast
PHOTOGRAPHY BY HAP SAKWA

FACING PAGE
MATTHIEU CHEMINEE
Heirloom ■ 2012
22.8 x 20.3 x 2.5 cm
Sterling silver, white gold,
semiprecious stones
PHOTOGRAPHY BY ANTHONY MCLEAN

PANDORA M. BARTHEN
Celtic Serpent Wedding Necklace ■ 2011
Centerpiece: 5 x 7.6 cm
18-karat gold, enamel, rose-cut diamonds, South
Sea cultured pearl; lost wax cast, guilloché
PHOTOGRAPHY BY LEE WOOLDRIDGE

EINA AHLUWALIA
Kirpan Necklace ■ 2011
Sword: 16 x 16 x 2 cm
Brass, 22-karat gold plate, silver plate;
fabricated, hand-saw pierced
PHOTOGRAPHY BY PRADIP PATRA

13

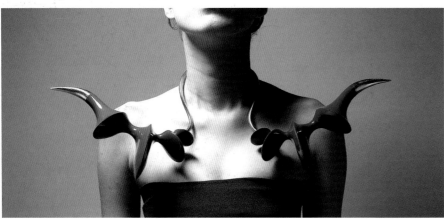

YUN SANGHEE
An Attack by Green Horns ■ 2009
24.9 x 57.2 x 7.4 cm
Korean lacquer, wood, sterling
silver, gold plating, gold leaf
PHOTOGRAPHY BY MUNCH STUDIO

PETRA CLASS
Green Arabesque Necklace ■ 2009

18 x 2 x 0.2 cm
Aquamarine, emerald, sapphire, tourmaline,
pearl, diamond, 22-karat and 18-karat gold
PHOTOGRAPHY BY HAP SAKWA

15

KATY HACKNEY
Rectangle and Circles Necklace ■ 2011
Pendant: 8 x 8 cm
Pear wood, boxwood, brass, silver, paint, found objects, graphite, cord; carved, fabricated
PHOTOGRAPHY BY SUSSIE AHLBURG

FACING PAGE
KATHLEEN NOWAK TUCCI
Camille Necklace ■ 2011
15 x 4 x 1.5 cm
Recycled motorcycle inner tubes, bronze metal clay, gilder's patina; hand cut
PHOTOGRAPHY BY ROBERT DIAMANTE

LAUREN BLAIS
The Botany of Nostalgia Series ■ 2008

Overall length: 71 cm
Silver, patina, silk, hair; hand
fabricated, etched, embroidered
PHOTOGRAPHY BY KAREN PHILLIPPI

DAVIDE BIGAZZI
Lancia Necklace ■ 2010
45 x 42 cm
Sterling silver, 18-karat gold;
oxidized, hand fabricated
PHOTOGRAPHY BY HAP SAKWA

HENG LEE
Gorgeous Surface I ■ 2011
33.5 x 20 x 26.5 cm
Silver wire copper plated
with platinum; pierced
PHOTOGRAPHY BY ARTIST

FACING PAGE
ANDREA WILLIAMS
Vinculum ■ 2012
68.5 x 7.6 x 7.6 cm
Found beach stones,
reclaimed sterling silver,
resin; carved, fabricated
PHOTOGRAPHY BY MARK CRAIG

ELIZABETH W. RUSNELL
Green Maples ■ 2011
46 x 6 x 2.5 cm
Handmade porcelain and polymer beads, glass beads,
linen cord; glazed, painted, knitted, macraméd
PHOTOGRAPHY BY JOE JUSTAD

AIMEE PETKUS
Co-Exist ■ 2011
35.5 x 20.3 x 5 cm
Copper; fold formed
PHOTOGRAPHY BY JOHN MCKINNON

SATOSHI NAKAMURA
Rose Collar ■ 2012
37 x 28 x 10 cm
Silk, iron, silver; lost wax cast
PHOTOGRAPHY BY ARTIST

LORENA N. BUENDIA
Nik ■ 2011
26 x 24 x 4 cm
Recycled cardboard, natural wool,
brass wire; felted, crimped
PHOTOGRAPHY BY PIOPICS

CHARLOTTE DE SYLLAS
Trumpet Necklace ■ 2011
Overall length: 41.2 cm
Synthetic ruby corundum,
22-karat and 18-karat gold;
carved, glued, riveted
PHOTOGRAPHY BY SIMON ARMITT

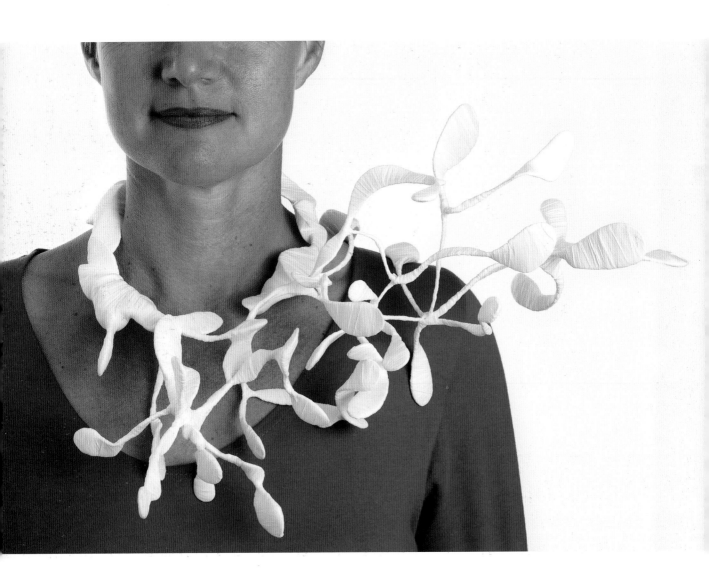

KARIN KORTENHORST
Always New ■ 2010
30 x 50 x 25 cm
Wire, plastic tape, wound
PHOTOGRAPHY BY ADRIAAN VAN DAM

YOSHIKO YAMAMOTO
570 Yards Necklace ■ 2012

30 x 30 x 5 cm
Nylon monofilament; hand crocheted
PHOTOGRAPHY BY TONY PETTINATO

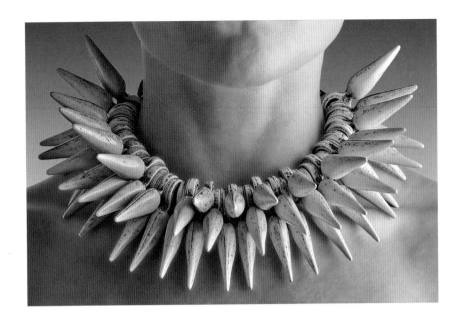

STEFANIE SHEEHAN
Scales Neckpiece ■ 2012
25.5 x 25.5 x 1.3 cm
Copper, paint, rubber cord; planished, formed
PHOTOGRAPHY BY MEREDITH BUGEL

SHARON ROSENTHAL
Necklace ■ 2012
25.4 cm wide
Lucite
PHOTOGRAPHY BY PETER GROESBECK

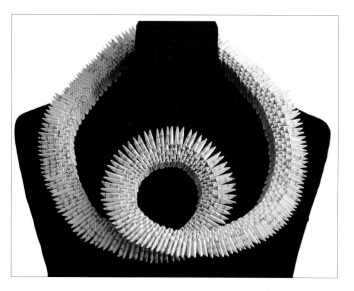
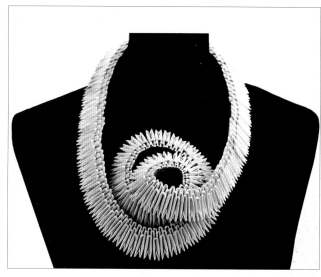

LITAL MENDEL
Just One More... ■ 2012
Overall length: 127 cm
Paper; origami
PHOTOGRAPHY BY NOA KEDMI

CHIHIRO MAKIO
Nouveau Necklace ■ 2010
26 x 18 x 5 cm
Sterling silver, onyx, embroidery thread, 24-karat
gold; fabricated, oxidized, hand crocheted
PHOTOGRAPHY BY IVO M. VERMEULEN

LAURA J. STAMPER
Aphrodite Art Necklace ■ 2012
50 x 6.5 x 1.5 cm
Porcelain, glaze, rough citrine, rubies, tourmaline,
topaz, sterling silver, 24-karat gold; sculpted, fired,
layered, burnished, cut, water cast, hand forged
PHOTOGRAPHY BY LARRY SANDERS

31

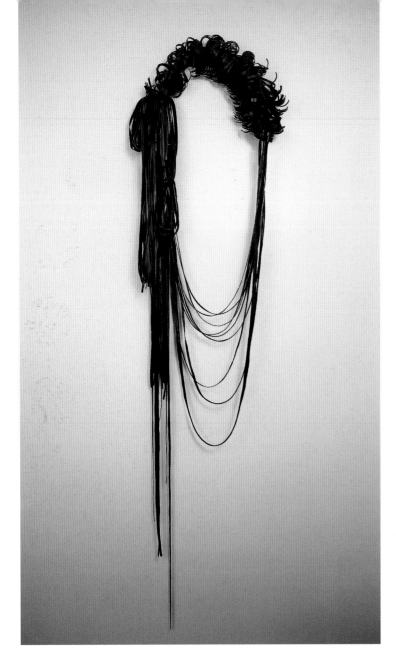

DANIEL MARCUCIO
Rubber Neckpiece ■ 2010
91.4 x 25.4 x 5.1 cm
Rubber; cut
PHOTOGRAPHY BY ABBY JOHNSTON

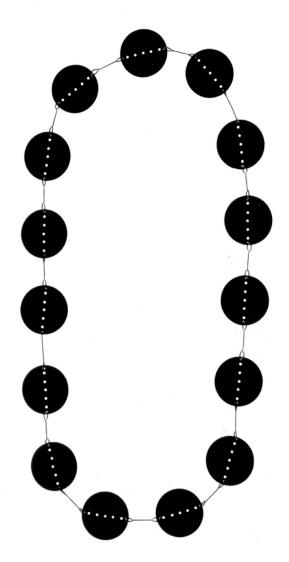

JOYCE ROESSLER
Cascade Necklace ■ 2010
30.4 x 20.3 x 2.5 cm
Glass, sterling silver; hand blown,
cut, shaped, and fabricated
PHOTOGRAPHY BY ROBERT DIAMANTE

TORE SVENSSON
Fifteen ■ 2010
28 x 14 x 5 cm
Steel, linseed oil; etched, soldered, fired
PHOTOGRAPHY BY FRANZ KARL

BIRTE SOELLNER
Untitled ■ 2012
33 x 15 x 2 cm
Stainless steel, leather, brass; gold plated, folded
PHOTOGRAPHY BY DANIEL WEISSER

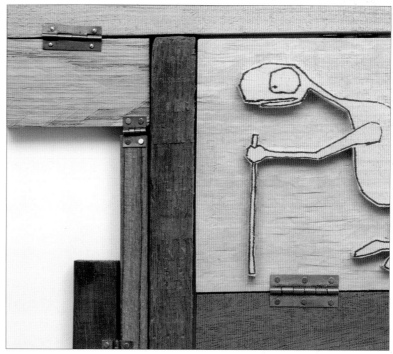

SIRJA KNAAPI
Untitled ■ 2012
51 x 20 x 2 cm
Wood, metal, fabric; handmade
PHOTOGRAPHY BY MIKKO J. SAVOLAINEN

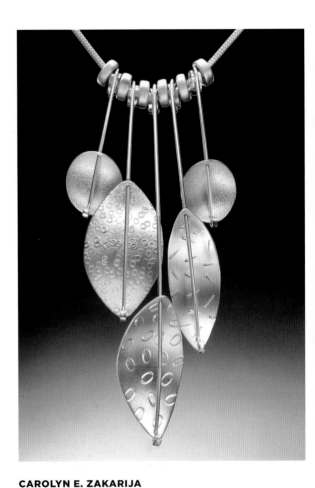

TODD REED
Sterling Silver Diamond Pendant ■ 2011
7 x 7 x 1.3 cm
Sterling silver, patina, white brilliant-cut
diamonds, raw diamond, 18-karat gold
PHOTOGRAPHY BY BRIAN MARK

CAROLYN E. ZAKARIJA
Falling Leaves ■ 2010
Leaves: 4.8 x 2.8 x 0.3 cm
Sterling silver, 14-karat gold; hand stamped
PHOTOGRAPHY BY RALPH GABRINER

SOOYOUNG KIM
Strombo Cactus ■ 2012
Pendant: 5.7 x 3.8 x 2.5 cm
Sterling silver, freshwater pearl; fabricated, chased,
repoussé, textured, soldered, hammered, oxidized
PHOTOGRAPHY BY ARTIST

SHIRLI MATATIA
Angel Wings Pendant ■ 2011
7 x 5 cm
Silver, plastic, pearls; cast,
fabricated, cut, textured, strung
PHOTOGRAPHY BY MARINA MOSHKOVICH

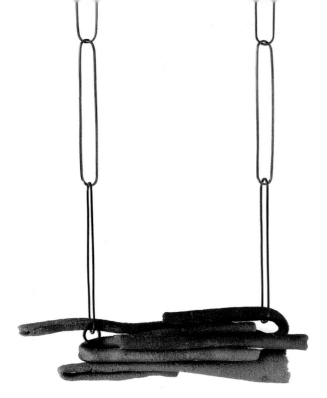

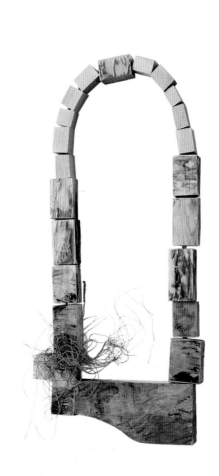

SUSAN K. SLOAN
Chain/Trumpets ■ 2010
45 x 18 x 2 cm
Epoxy resin, pigments, sterling silver
PHOTOGRAPHY BY STEVEN B. SAMUELS

ANNA VAN DE POL DE DEUS
Just Let It Out ■ 2012
40 x 15.5 x 2.4 cm
Beech wood, thread; image transfer
PHOTOGRAPHY BY FEDERICO CAVICCHIOLI

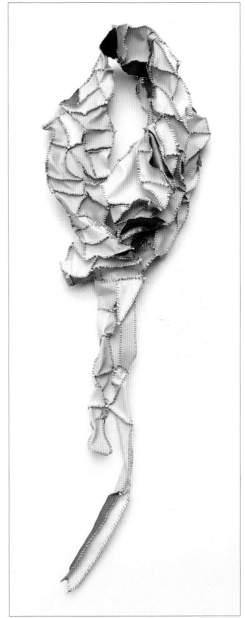

DOROTHÉE VAN BIESEN
Rose-Blanc-Doré ■ 2012
67 x 23 x 10 cm
Leather-like material; hand stitched
PHOTOGRAPHY BY ARTIST

MARGHERITA DE MARTINO NORANTE
Be Careful Clementine #2 ■ 2009
55 x 10 x 4 cm
Silver, cotton, wool, plastic beads;
hand formed and sewed
PHOTOGRAPHY BY ARTIST

ALEXANDRA PEREZ DEMMA
Chittagong 1 ■ 2012
81.2 x 33 x 5 cm
Steel, copper, found rope; fabricated,
chased, repoussé, rusted
PHOTOGRAPHY BY SETH PAPAC

MELISSA CABLE
Time of My Life ■ 2011
Pendant: 8.8 x 7.6 x 2.5 cm
Plastic, acrylic, copper, brass, steel,
glass, watch parts, oil
PHOTOGRAPHY BY DOUG YAPLE

LORENA LAZARD
Acanthus Mollis V ■ 2012

Centerpiece: 11.5 x 11.5 x 0.5 cm
Sterling silver, 18-karat gold bimetal, shibuishi,
copper, iron, polymer clay, acrylic; image transfer

Showcase 500
art necklaces

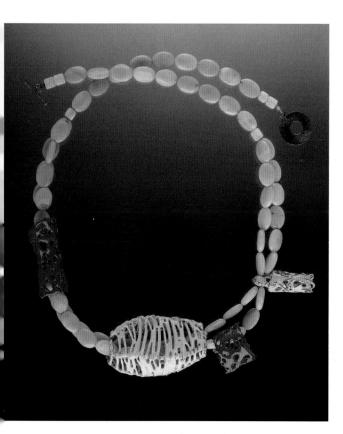

LIZ A. SCHOCK
Haiku ■ 2011
55.9 x 17.8 x 5.1 cm
Sterling silver, copper, enamel, lime jade,
aventurine; oxidized, fabricated, strung
PHOTOGRAPHY BY DEAN POWELL

JEONGHYE PARK
Growing ■ 2010
60 x 17 x 4.5 cm
Copper, fabric; fabricated, painted
PHOTOGRAPHY BY MYUNG-WOOK HUH

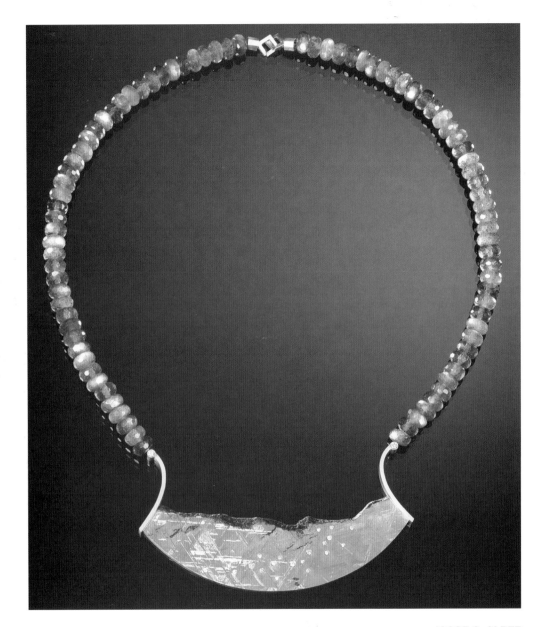

JACOB S. ALBEE
Embla Necklace ■ 2011
20 x 20 x 1.2 cm
Gibeon meteorite, 18-karat gold, labradorite,
diamonds; fabricated, etched
PHOTOGRAPHY BY EXTANT PHOTOGRAPHY

Showcase 500
art necklaces

NOÉMIE DOGE
Handle ■ 2011
70 x 30 x 4.5 cm
Sterling silver, pewter, silver plate; linked
PHOTOGRAPHY BY BAPTISTE COULON AND SANDRA POINTET

49

MOLLY GINNELLY
LORRAINE ROBSON
Ceramic and Silver Neckpiece ■ 2012
60 x 2 x 2 cm
Ceramic, silver, 18-karat gold, sterling silver;
fabricated, inlaid, formed, fired, diamond polished

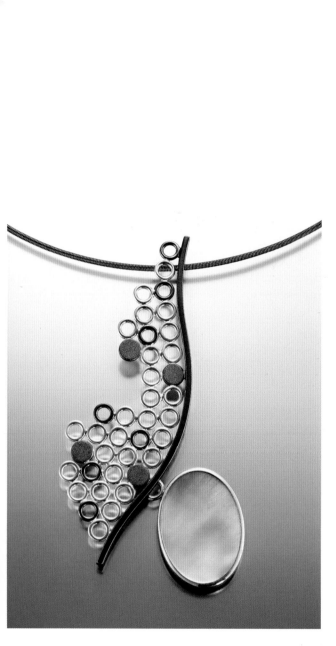

JANIS KERMAN
Untitled ■ 2010

Pendant: 7 x 2.5 x 0.2 cm
Sterling silver, 18-karat gold,
mother-of-pearl; oxidized
PHOTOGRAPHY BY DALE GOULD

SYDNEY LYNCH
Night Forest Necklace ■ 2012

Pendant cluster: 7.6 cm long
Silver, 18-karat gold, tourmalines, labradorite,
Tahitian pearl, quartz briolette; oxidized, fabricated
PHOTOGRAPHY BY ALAN JACKSON

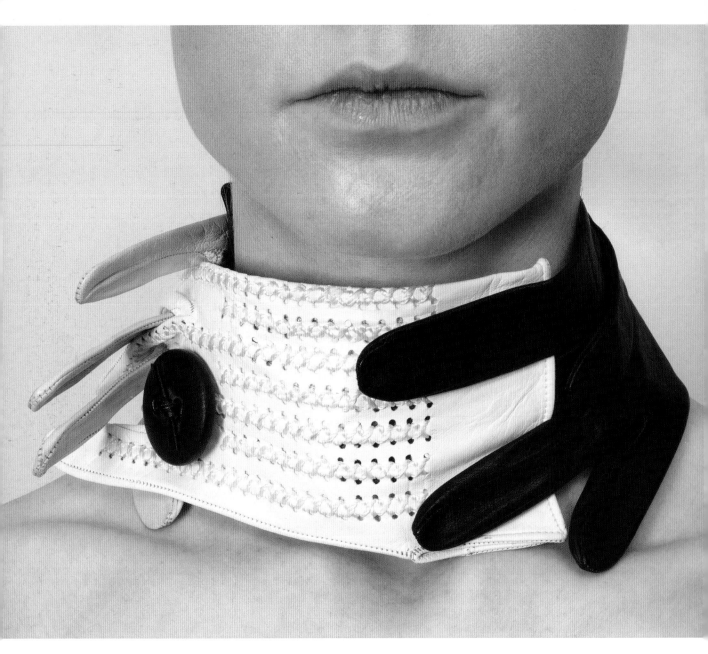

ELIDA KEMELMAN
Hands I ■ 2012
9 x 51 x 0.5 cm
Leather gloves, leather button,
magnets; constructed
PHOTOGRAPHY BY DAMIÁN WASSER

BARBARA COHEN
Balloon Necklace ■ 2010
22 x 22 x 5 cm
Balloons, rubber, pearls; fabricated
PHOTOGRAPHY BY ARTIST

53

CAROLE GRISHAM
Creamsicle ■ 2012
18 x 1.3 x 1.3 cm
Vintage German Lucite barrel beads, Japanese glass
seed beads, wooden bead forms, gold findings
PHOTOGRAPHY BY DOUGLAS EVANS

ANN TEVEPAUGH MITCHELL
Green Man ■ 2012
26 x 20 x 3 cm
Glass beads, thread; dimensional peyote and
fringe techniques, improvised stitching
PHOTOGRAPHY BY DEAN POWELL

CAROLE HORN
Titania's Garland of Leaves ■ 2011
Overall length: 48 cm
Seed beads; peyote stitch, herringbone stitch
PHOTOGRAPHY BY D. JAMES DEE

IRINA RUDNEVA
Manhattan Night Lights ■ 2011
38.1 x 22.8 x 2.5 cm
Japanese beads, rhinestones, black
onyx beads; bead embroidered
PHOTOGRAPHY BY VALERY BYDZAN

Showcase 500
art necklaces

IRINA ASTRATENKO
Solaris ■ 2012

32 x 17 cm
Seed beads, Swarovski crystals, polyester
thread; beadwork, Ankars technique

HELI KAUHANEN
Boforia Seasons:
Autumn ■ 2011

30 x 30 x 15 cm
Anodized titanium
PHOTOGRAPHY BY TEEMU TÖYRYLÄ

ADRIENNE GASKELL
Alexandra Necklace ■ 2009

50 x 2.5 cm
Precious metal beads, Swarovski crystals,
Czech glass beads, sterling-silver wire;
needle woven, wire fabrication
PHOTOGRAPHY BY HAP SAKWA

DIANA VINCENT
Spiral Oxidized Sterling-Silver Necklace ■ 2012
2.5 x 2.5 x 2.5 cm
Sterling silver; handmade, oxidized
PHOTOGRAPHY BY ARTIST

JENNY LLEWELLYN
Plume Necklace ■ 2011
40 x 5 x 5 cm
Luminescent silicone,
18-karat gold-plated silver

MARTY JONAS
Spirals ■ 2012
30 x 21.5 x 2.5 cm
Silk thread; hand dyed, crocheted
PHOTOGRAPHY BY ARTIST

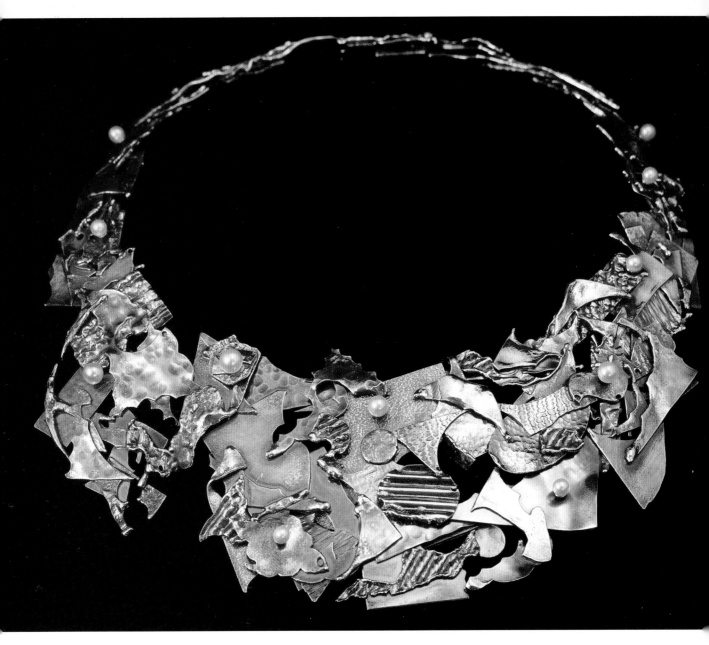

GHINA MACHKHAS
Seeking Serenity ■ 2012
20 x 18 cm
Sterling silver, cultured white pearls;
textured, oxidized, hand fabricated
PHOTOGRAPHY BY DRAGOS DOROBANTU

TIA KRAMER
Necklace from the Fluttering Series ■ 2011
36 x 4 x 1.5 cm
Sterling silver, handmade waterproof paper; oxidized
PHOTOGRAPHY BY HANK DREW

DONALD A. BEAUBIER
Untitled ■ 2011
Pendant: 7 x 5 x 1.5 cm
Sterling silver, amethyst; fabricated, textured
PHOTOGRAPHY BY ERIC WALSH

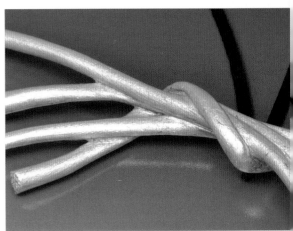

KRISTIN D. LEVIER
Sprig Necklace ■ 2012
Pendant: 22 x 15 x 1 cm
European pear wood, compressed beech,
silver leaf, acrylic paint; carved, bent
PHOTOGRAPHY BY JONATHAN BILLINGS ARCHER

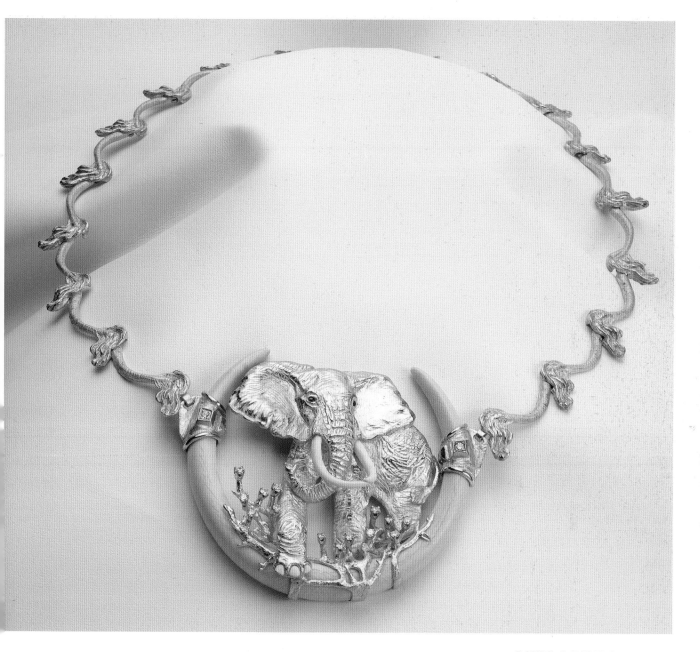

DANIEL C. TOLEDO
Golden Tusker ■ 2010
26.7 x 21 x 1.3 cm
22-karat yellow gold, 18-karat yellow gold,
fossilized mammoth ivory, rubies, diamonds
PHOTOGRAPHY BY STEVE GILLHAM

65

HEIDEMARIE HERB
Network 2012 ■ 2012
Overall length: 75 cm
Brass, wire, melted pigments, sterling silver
PHOTOGRAPHY BY SILVANA TILI

HANNA L. HEDMAN
While They Await Extinction ■ 2011
36 x 17 x 9 cm
Silver, copper, paint; fabricated, pierced,
soldered, oxidized, powder coated
PHOTOGRAPHY BY SANNA LINDBERG

AMBER O'HARROW
Knitter's Necklace ■ 2009
56 x 20 x 8 cm
Anodized aluminum and copper
wire, wool; knitted, hand spun
PHOTOGRAPHY BY ARTIST

ANNE FIALA
Keeping My Regrets ■ 2011
36.8 x 19 x 5.8 cm
Wood, steel, brass, silver,
cotton string, cotton
PHOTOGRAPHY BY ARTIST

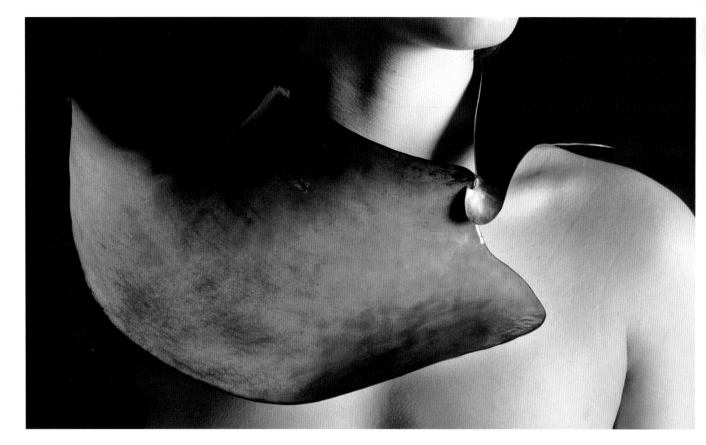

DANIELLE M. GERBER
Water ■ 2011

23 x 33 x 20 cm
Brass, enameled copper
PHOTOGRAPHY BY KATIE TRUCHON

VINCENT VAN HEES
ONI ■ 2010

15 x 14 x 0.7 cm
18-karat yellow gold; rolled, bent, laser welded,
stone-tension set, matte finished, polished
PHOTOGRAPHY BY ARTIST

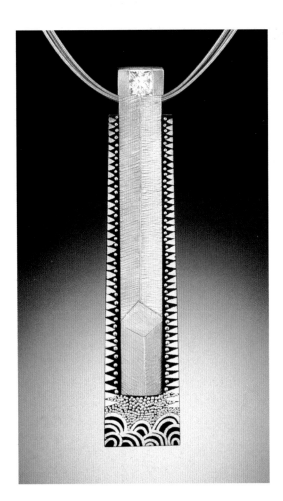

NAMU CHO

Mirage 8 ■ 2005

Pendant: 5.5 x 1 x 0.3 cm
24-karat gold, 22-karat gold,
steel, princess-cut diamond;
damascene and fusing techniques
PHOTOGRAPHY BY HAP SAKWA

BARBARA UMBEL

Floating Moon Snail Necklace ■ 2012

Pendant: 7.6 x 6.3 x 1.3 cm
14-karat yellow gold, sterling silver, Atlantic
moon snail, Australian boulder opal, volte
and freshwater pearls; forged, fabricated
PHOTOGRAPHY BY RYDER GLEDHILL

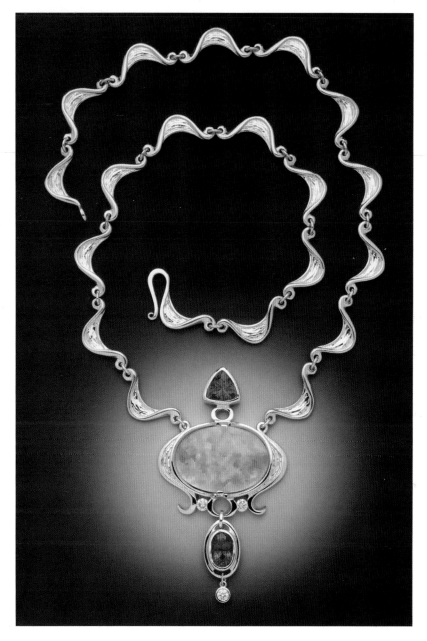

GLENN R. DIZON
Fit for a Queen ■ 2010
43.1 x 5.8 x 0.5 cm
14-karat gold, opal, spessartite,
pink spinel, diamonds
PHOTOGRAPHY BY GEORGE POST

71

MARIA LURO
Between Heaven and Earth ■ 2011
30 x 20 x 2 cm
Sterling silver, copper, nickel silver,
paper, wire; fused, constructed
PHOTOGRAPHY BY DAMIÁN WASSER

TOM FERRERO
Fractured ■ 2012
Pendant: 8 x 5 x 2 cm
Sterling silver, copper, steel, citrine,
peridot, rutilated quartz
PHOTOGRAPHY BY ARTIST

73

JANICE HO
Acid to Alkaline ■ 2011
7.6 x 6.8 x 1.2 cm
Sterling silver, enamel, copper, test
tubes, cork; fabricated, torch fired
PHOTOGRAPHY BY ARTIST

JIYE YUN
Heart 2 ■ 2011
20 x 16 x 2 cm
Stainless steel, sterling silver,
paint marker; riveted, drawn
PHOTOGRAPHY BY MYUNG-WOOK HUH

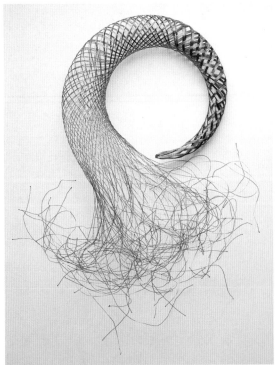

KRISZTINA NÉMETH
Time Jewel ■ 2010
40 x 23 x 13 cm
Metal string, gold
PHOTOGRAPHY BY APOR PÜSPÖKI

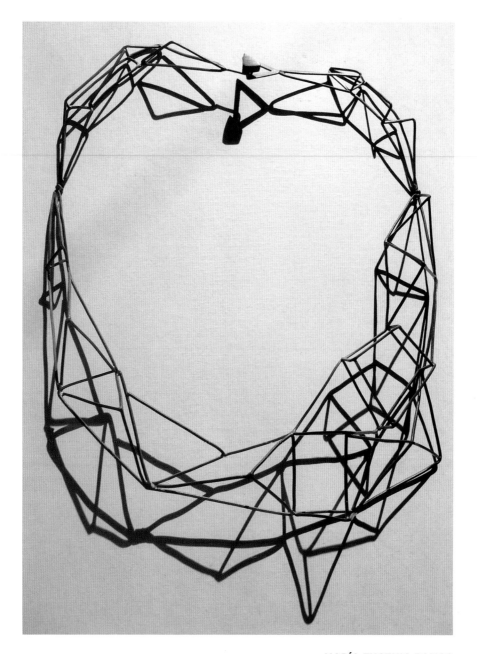

MARÍA EUGENIA RAMOS
Networks ■ 2012
20 x 17 x 4 cm
Alpaca, oxidized
PHOTOGRAPHY BY ARTIST

77

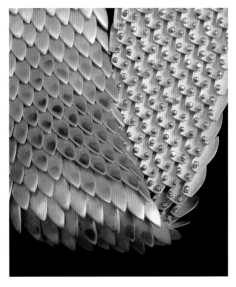

JON M. RYAN
Untitled ■ 2009
156 x 5 x 0.5 cm
Sterling silver,
18-karat gold;
cast, fabricated

MICHAEL BANNER
MAUREEN BANNER
Ionic Collar #4 ■ 2011

28 x 28 x 2.5 cm
Sheet silver, enamel; cloisonné, hammered, anticlastic raising, shell
formed, fabricated, constructed, hollow formed, soldered, linked
PHOTOGRAPHY BY JOHN POLAK

PETER HOOGEBOOM
Westland ■ 2011
64 x 3.2 x 3.2 cm
Terra cotta, silver, nylon; silversmithing
PHOTOGRAPHY BY FRANCIS WILLEMSTIJN

SE HEE UM

Necklace ■ 2012

47 x 5 x 0.9 cm
Concrete, sterling silver, seedlings, brass, silk, ramie
fabric; molded, oxidized, linked, fabricated, soldered
PHOTOGRAPHY BY STUDIO MUNCH

81

THOMAS W. TURNER
Amethyst Necklace ■ 2012
Pendant: 7.6 x 1.7 x 1.3 cm
18-karat gold, amethyst, diamonds,
rhodolite garnet; fabricated
AMETHYST BY TOM MUNSTEINER
PHOTOGRAPHY BY HAP SAKWA

SAMARA M. CHRISTIAN
Phoenix Pendant ■ 2012

42 x 45 x 11 cm
14-karat white gold, 14-karat rose gold, white
diamonds, champagne diamond, carved
agate; pavé set, bezel set, lost wax cast
PHOTOGRAPHY BY CHRIS ADYNIEC

83

RICHARD LINDSAY
Inuit Wand Collar ■ 2010

39.3 x 23.6 x 1.9 cm
Sterling-silver mixed wire, sterling-silver pod, 14-karat gold
balls, rusted steel knife, brass, sterling silver, copper, blue
topaz, fossilized walrus bone, sponge coral, crystal; riveted
PHOTOGRAPHY BY HAP SAKWA

SO YOUNG PARK
Bubble Fruit ▪ 2010

Pendant: 6 x 4 x 1 cm
Silver, carnelian, citrine, green
onyx; chased, soldered, oxidized
PHOTOGRAPHY BY ARTIST

LESLEY MESSAM
Fantasyland Necklace ▪ 2011

Pendant: 6.3 x 3.8 x 3.8 cm
Ceramic clay, metal clay paste, sterling
silver, lampworked beads, patina;
hand fabricated, fired, soldered
PHOTOGRAPHY BY ABBY JOHNSON

85

PILAR AGUECI
Untitled ■ 2012

40 x 40 x 6 cm
Found objects, silk cord; naturally weathered
PHOTOGRAPHY BY NADIA ZHENG

KATE SIBLEY
From the Fast Fashion Collection:
Double Fold Pink ■ 2012

40 x 15 x 2 cm
Paper derived from stone, vegetable
ink, gold leaf; hand cut, folded
PHOTOGRAPHY BY ARTIST

87

UOSIS JUODVALKIS
JACQUELYN RICE
Kite Necklace ■ 2010

55.8 x 40.6 x 2.5 cm
Bronze, sterling silver;
cast, oxidized, antiqued
PHOTOGRAPHY BY ARTISTS

EVELYN MARKASKY
Dentata ■ 2012

Group of pendants: 5.9 x 1.2 x 0.1 cm
Copper, enamels; torch fired, pierced,
formed, handmade, fused
PHOTOGRAPHY BY ARTIST

ERIN PRAIS-HINTZ
Old Love ■ 2012

20 x 1 x 1 cm
Precious metal clay, copper bezel, keishi
pearls, crystals, river stones, resin
PHOTOGRAPHY BY JOHN HARTMAN

MYUNG URSO

Floating ■ 2012

30 x 19 x 7 cm
Silk, cotton fabric, sterling-silver
wire; hand sewn, lacquered

JENNIFER J. FECKER

Crystal Dot Neckpiece ■ 2011

22.3 x 20.3 x 0.7 cm
Wool felt, Swarovski crystals; hand cut, assembled

Showcase 500
art necklaces

**R-BOLT + J-CRACK
(RACHEL TIMMINS AND JUSTIN MAGES)**
ARGH! Pirates! ■ 2012
40.6 x 38.1 x 7.6 cm
Spandex, thread, polyester
stuffing, water-based ink
PHOTOGRAPHY BY JOSEPH HYDE

JEONG-SUN CHOI
H2O.03 ■ 2010
23 x 24 x 10 cm
Sterling silver, nylon, plastic
PHOTOGRAPHY BY MYUNG-WOOK HUH

SUMIKO HATTORI
Color Shadow Pendants ▪ 2011
Each: 8 x 6 x 4.5 cm
Paint, silver, stainless steel
PHOTOGRAPHY BY ARTIST

Showcase 500
art necklaces

MONICA CHOI
Architectural Work on Human Body ■ 2012

Pendant frame: 6 x 4 x 1.5 cm
Silver base metal, 18-karat white and yellow gold plate, turquoise,
amethyst, jade, magnets, steel bars; mounted, textured, carved
PHOTOGRAPHY BY MYUNG-WOOK HUH

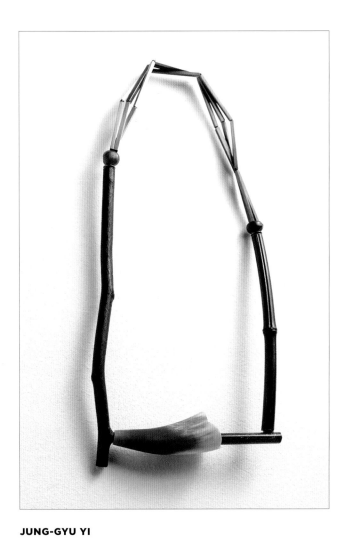

ELLIOT C. GASKIN
Serpent's Head ■ 2012

39.4 x 6.4 x 1.3 cm
Bone, brass, sterling silver,
nickel silver, ruby
PHOTOGRAPHY BY ARTIST

JUNG-GYU YI
Necklace 2 ■ 2011

46 x 20 x 4 cm
Horn, branch, lacquered bamboo,
dried seed, sterling silver; oxidized
PHOTOGRAPHY BY KWANGCHOON PARK

CHRISTINE DEMMEL
Phoenix's Nest ■ 2012
55 x 4.5 cm
Ceramic, sterling silver, iron,
feathers, nylon; hand shaped,
raku fired, chased, mounted

GREGORY LARIN
Gory Story ■ 2010
50.8 x 43.1 x 10.1 cm
Polymer, sterling silver
PHOTOGRAPHY BY ALEX KUCHERENKO

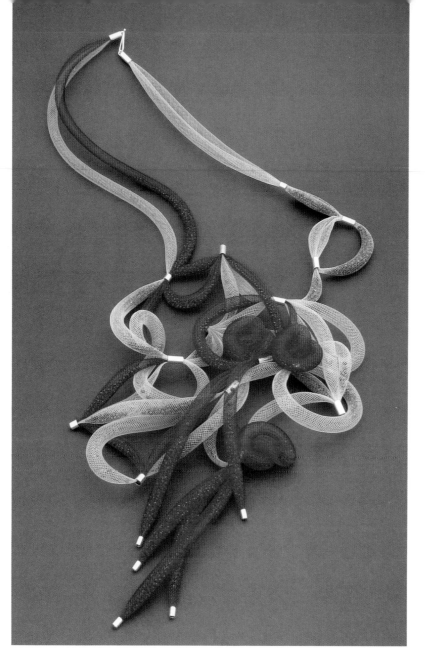

ANNEMARIE MATZAKOW
Popsy-Wopsy ■ 2012
60 x 19 x 4 cm
Polyester monofilament, sterling silver,
glass beads; heat shaped, sewed
PHOTOGRAPHY BY ARTIST

NAMU CHO
Sprite Wrap ▓ 2012

16 x 15 x 2 cm
24-karat gold, steel, diamonds;
damascene and fusing techniques
PHOTOGRAPHY BY HAP SAKWA

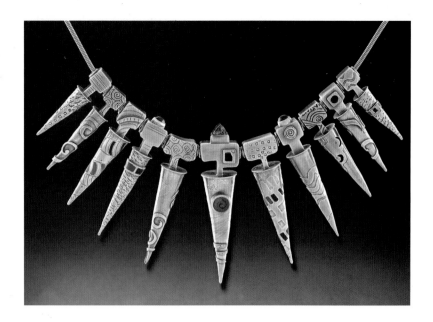

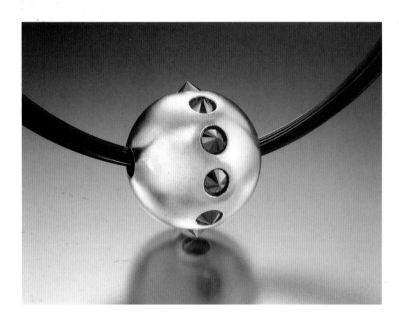

JEANNIE HWANG
Wandering Star ■ 2011

Pendant: 1.5 cm in diameter
14-karat white gold, black
diamonds, coated steel cable
PHOTOGRAPHY BY HAP SAKWA

GREG JORDAN
BJ JORDAN
Warrior Collar ■ 2011

Row of cone forms: 8.9 x 30.4 cm
Sterling silver, brass, polymer clay, lapis, amethyst, and
tourmaline; oxidized, hand constructed, acid etched
PHOTOGRAPHY BY LARRY SANDERS

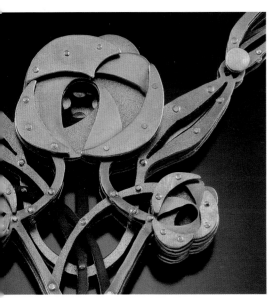

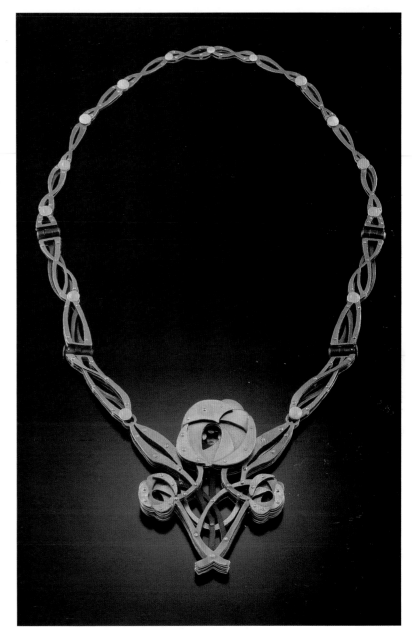

DOUGLAS E. WUNDER
The Metallic Rose ■ 2012
20 x 15 x 1 cm
Titanium, silver, 24-karat gold;
hand sawed, constructed, cold
connected, soldered, riveted
PHOTOGRAPHY BY LARRY SANDERS

101

RUANN EWING
Beads and Iron ▪ 2011
25 x 15 x 2.5 cm
Iron rod, sterling-silver rod, glass beads;
hammered, forged, woven
PHOTOGRAPHY BY JOE WHITTKOP

MARGO C. FIELD
Dogwood and Pussy Willows ■ 2012
22 x 15 x 1 cm
Seed beads, glass pearls, crystals, Czech glass
beads, copper hook, beading thread; peyote
stitch, herringbone stitch, invented stitches
PHOTOGRAPHY BY PAT BERRETT

LYNN COBB
Silver Flower with Gold ■ 2010
Flower: 5 cm in diameter
Metal clay; molded, hand formed,
kiln fired, burnished, tumbled
PHOTOGRAPHY BY GEORGE POST

103

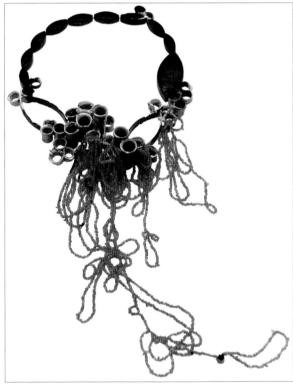

KATIE L. POTERALA
From the Affliction Series: 01015 ■ 2012
66 x 30.5 x 6.3 cm
Brass, seed beads; powder coated
PHOTOGRAPHY BY TIFFINEY YAZZIE

SHARMINI U. WIRASEKARA
Butterflies ■ 2011
43 x 31 cm
Glass Delica seed beads, round seed beads,
crystal beads; peyote stitch, right-angle weave
PHOTOGRAPHY BY BARBARA COHEN

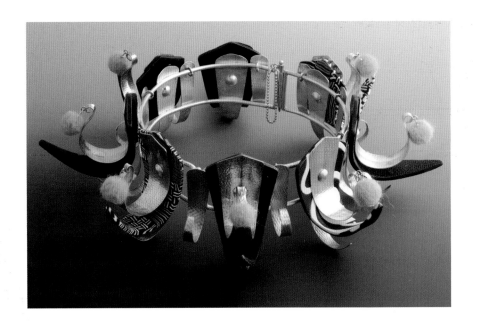

DIANA M. DIEBOLD
Jester's Choker ■ 2011
6 x 22 x 5.5 cm
Sterling-silver wire and sheet, polymer clay, wool; felted, fabricated
PHOTOGRAPHY BY PETER U. DIEBOLD

MARIANNE HUNTER
2600 Mosaics of Galaxies ■ 2012
1.6 x 9.1 x 0.4 cm
24-karat gold, 14-karat gold enamel over foils, opal, diamonds, emerald cabochon, sapphire, rutilated quartz over parrot feathers, sphalerite; carved, fabricated, engraved
PHOTOGRAPHY BY GEORGE POST

SANDRA J. MATASICK
Comfrey ■ 2010
Pendant: 6 x 7.5 x 1.5 cm
Pink tourmaline, diamonds, Tahitian pearl,
18-karat yellow gold; cast, hand constructed
PHOTOGRAPHY BY HAP SAKWA

DANIEL P. STEVENS
Gold Pod Necklace ■ 2011
22.8 x 13.4 x 2 cm
18-karat gold, 22-karat gold, sterling silver, rose-cut
labradorite; fabricated, fused, soldered, blackened
PHOTOGRAPHY BY ELIZABETH LAMARK

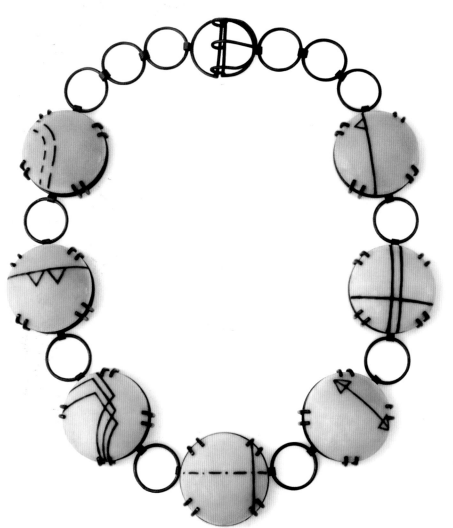

ABIGAIL W. HEUSS
Kay ■ 2012
45.7 x 3 x 1.2 cm
Copper, tin, enamel, patina;
fabricated, sawed, set
PHOTOGRAPHY BY ARTIST

SUZAN REZAC

A Dozen Roses ▓ 2011

49 x 3 x 1.5 cm
Sterling silver, brass, shakudo,
18-karat gold, shibuichi;
constructed, inlaid
PHOTOGRAPHY BY TOM VAN EYNDE

NORA ROCHEL
Herbalism ■ 2011
50 x 6 x 5 cm
Silver, bronze, aluminum;
oxidized, lost wax cast
PHOTOGRAPHY BY ARTIST

TAMARA GRÜNER
Jais Scarabee ■ 2012
Pendant: 11.5 x 18.5 x 1.3 cm
Historical metal plate, glass,
mother-of-pearl, silver, onyx;
blackened, mounted
PHOTOGRAPHY BY ARTIST

111

LAURIE DANCH
Red Ribbon Collar ■ 2010

50.8 x 30.4 x 7.6 cm
Silk ribbon, silk dupioni,
crystals, glass beads, pearls
PHOTOGRAPHY BY MARTIN KONOPACKI

Showcase 500
art necklaces

SEUNG-HEA LEE
Floral Power ■ 2011

50 x 6.5 x 3 cm
Silver, rubies, peridote, crystal,
multi-tourmaline, citrine, turquoise;
oxidized, fabricated
PHOTOGRAPHY BY MYUNG-WOOK HUH

DEB KARASH
Gift ■ 2012

9.5 x 6.5 x 0.5 cm
Sterling silver, copper, brass, colored
pencils, diamonds; fabricated
PHOTOGRAPHY BY LARRY SANDERS

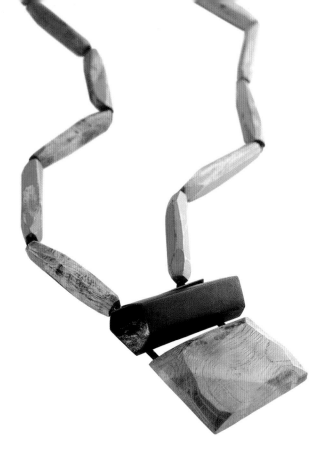

CRISTINA ZANI
My Seoul Necklace ■ 2012

52 x 6 x 3 cm
Copper, brass, patina, 24-karat gold leaf, wood,
acrylic paint, linen thread, patina; fabricated
PHOTOGRAPHY BY SHANNON TAFT

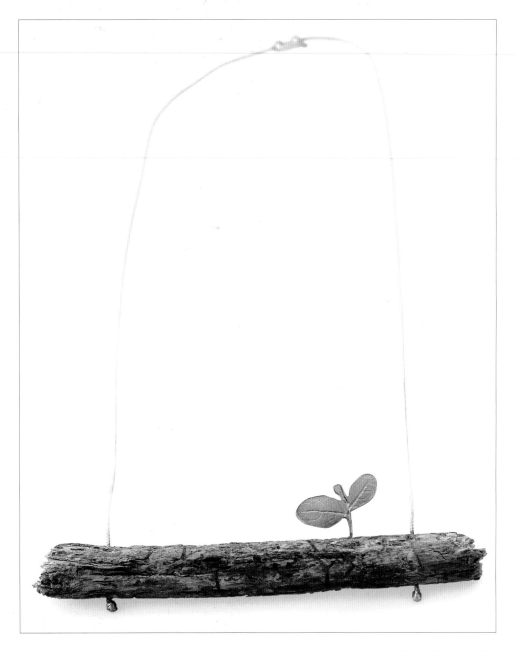

ANNE CASTELLANOS
Life ■ 2011
25 x 11.5 x 1.4 cm
Sterling silver, wood; lost
wax cast, fabricated
PHOTOGRAPHY BY ARTIST

115

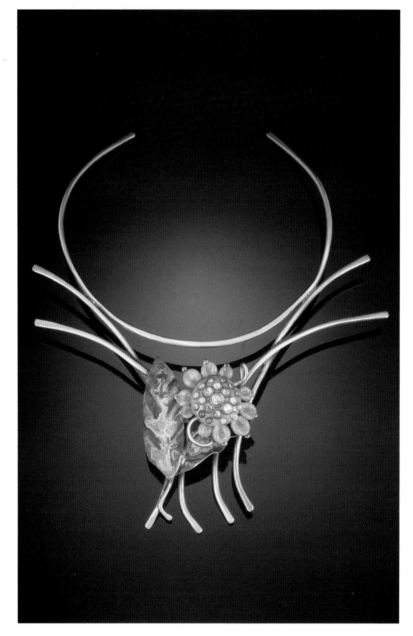

CYNDIE S. SMITH
The Garden Necklace ■ 2010
41 x 15 x 0.5 cm
Brass wire, copper sheet, bead,
patina; lampworked, fabricated,
hammered, sawed, folded, soldered

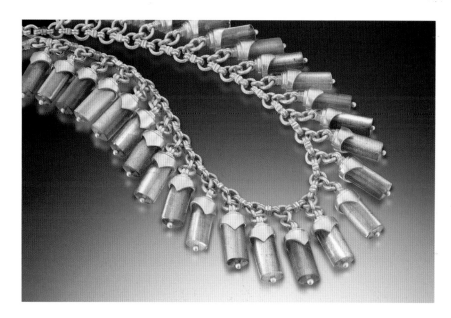

LILLY A. FITZGERALD
Labradorite Necklace ■ 2012

60.9 cm long
22-karat gold, labradorite
cylinders; cast, hand built, set
PHOTOGRAPHY BY HAP SAKWA

K. CLAIRE MACDONALD
Magnified 01 ■ 2011

Pendant: 5.5 x 8 x 1.5 cm
Wood, brass, steel, paint, cord;
painted, fabricated, repoussé
PHOTOGRAPHY BY ARTIST

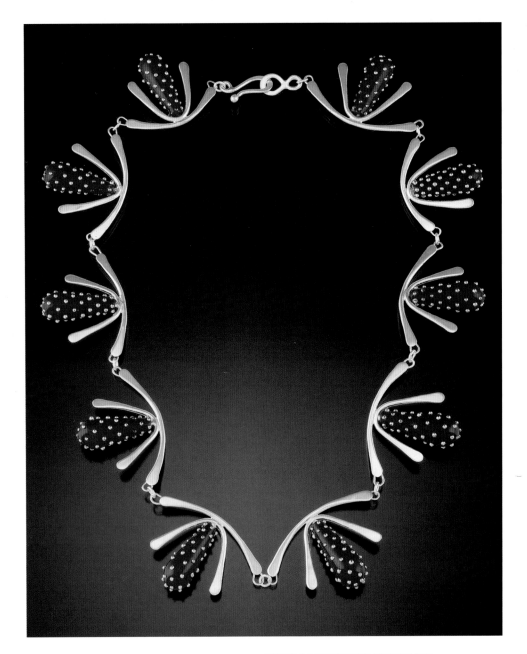

PATRICIA ZABRESKI VENALECK
Fire ■ 2011
Overall length: 50.8 cm
Sterling silver, wire, effetre
glass, reduction glass; forged,
soldered, torch formed
PHOTOGRAPHY BY LARRY SANDERS

SANDRA SCHUMANN
Resin Neckpiece ◼ 2012
40.6 x 27.9 x 3.8 cm
Brass, palladium, resin, fabric
PHOTOGRAPHY BY PETRA JASCHKE

KARINA GUEVIN
Purple Magnolia ■ 2012
48.2 x 12.7 x 12.7 cm
Glass; flameworked
PHOTOGRAPHY BY ARTIST

JENNY LLEWELLYN
Plume Necklace Glowing ■ 2011
40 x 5 x 5 cm
Luminescent silicone, silver
PHOTOGRAPHY BY JENNY LLEWELLYN

JEONG-SUN CHOI
H2O.01 ■ 2010
26 x 22 x 6.5 cm
Sterling silver, nylon, plastic
PHOTOGRAPHY BY MYUNG-WOOK HUH

SUSANNE KLEMM
Pearleater ■ 2012
40.6 x 40.6 x 10.1 cm
Polyolefin, freshwater pearls
PHOTOGRAPHY BY ARTIST

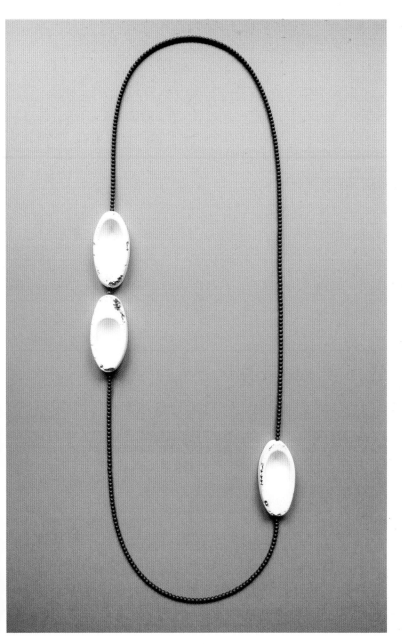

MELANIE BLESSMANN
Concrete with Steel ■ 2011
45 x 10 x 2 cm
Concrete, steel balls, hematite
PHOTOGRAPHY BY ARTIST

KATRINA M. VIRGONA
Oscillator | Mescalator | Stipulator ■ 2012
Each: 24 x 15 x 3 cm
Merino wool, stainless steel chain; hand felted
PHOTOGRAPHY BY BEN JOEL

MISUN WON
Jogakbo Wrapping Necklace ■ 2011
35 x 25 x 1.8 cm
Sterling silver, cord; hand cut
PHOTOGRAPHY BY ARTIST

VIKTORIA MUENZKER
Abyssal Art ■ 2012
50 x 10 x 5 cm
Driftwood, plastic beads, cotton thread, brass,
cyan ink; painted, pierced, sewed, threaded
PHOTOGRAPHY BY ARTIST

MELANIE A. MUIR
*Symphony in Monochrome
and Fuchsia* ■ 2011

84 x 6 x 2 cm
Polymer, beads, mokume
gane; hollow formed
PHOTOGRAPHY BY EWEN WEATHERSPOON

FACING PAGE
JEE HYE KWON
Airy ■ 2011
25.4 x 30.4 x 8.8 cm
Silver, tourmaline, diamonds,
kunzite; oxidized
PHOTOGRAPHY BY RALPH GABRINER

Showcase 500
art necklaces

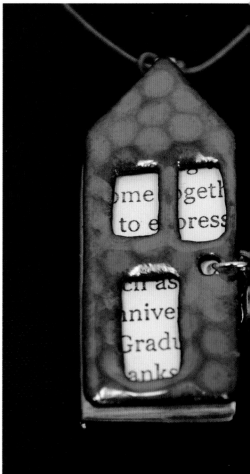

JEAN VAN BREDERODE
LYNNE SUPROCK
Enameled House Book Necklace ■ 2012
Book pendant: 3.8 x 2.5 cm
Copper, enamel, cardstock, plastic lacing
PHOTOGRAPHY BY LYNNE SUPROCK

ANDREW DANYLEWICH
Jealous Sea ■ 2012
Pendant: 3 x 2.5 cm
Overall length: 48 cm
Sterling silver, tourmaline; fabricated
PHOTOGRAPHY BY ARTIST

129

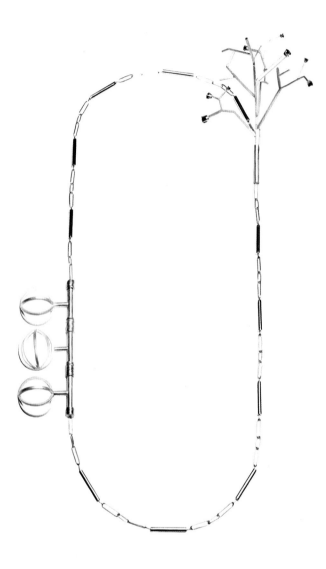

SUSAN J. CROSS
Ric Rac ■ 2010
28 x 25 cm
Silver tubing; threaded
PHOTOGRAPHY BY JOHN MCGREGOR

KRISTEN BAIRD
Through the Fence ■ 2011
35 x 16 x 9 cm
Sterling silver, garnet; fabricated
PHOTOGRAPHY BY JOHN MCKINNON

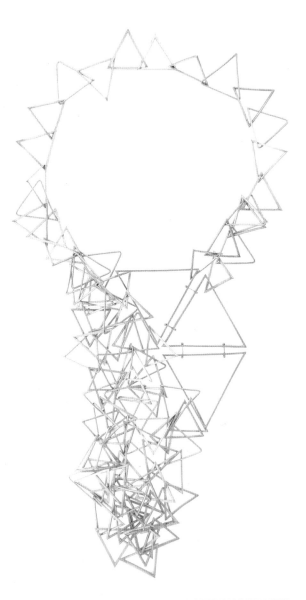

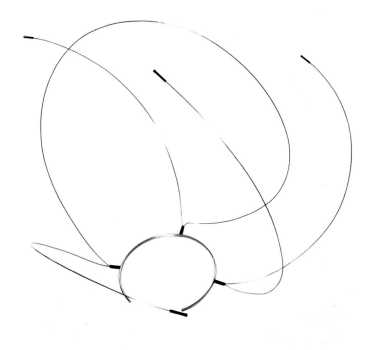

LOUISE MAKOWSKI
Cornered ■ 2012
38.1 x 12.7 x 1.3 cm
Sterling-silver wire; hand fabricated
PHOTOGRAPHY BY ARTIST

DOMINIQUE THOMAS
Untitled ■ 2012
40 x 45 x 45 cm
Sterling silver, rubber;
hand fabricated
PHOTOGRAPHY BY ARTIST

131

CHIEN CHING LIAO
The Sequence of Bloom I ■ 2012
37 x 20 x 8 cm
Brass, copper, patina, colored
pencil; fold formed, fabricated
PHOTOGRAPHY BY ARTIST

JUN HU
Brain under the Red Flag ■ 2012
42 x 30 x 3 cm
Brass, textile; soldered
PHOTOGRAPHY BY ARTIST

SIAN BOSTWICK
Wonderland Neckpiece ■ 2010

33 x 22 cm
Leather, moonstone, garnet, gold-plated silver;
hand pierced, stitched, cut, riveted, fabricated,
raised, beaded, laser welded and soldered
PHOTOGRAPHY BY MIKE BLISSETT

Showcase 500
art necklaces

ALICE BO-WEN CHANG

Bodyspace/Bodyscape
Necklace ■ 2011

45 x 17 x 4.5 cm
Silver, copper, gold-plated copper;
oxidized, photo etched
PHOTOGRAPHY BY ARTIST

135

TIFFANY ROWE
Walking on Eggs ▪ 2012
21 x 20 x 12 cm
Eggshells, synthetic
pearls, nylon thread
PHOTOGRAPHY BY ARTIST

DOUG BUCCI
Islet ▪ 2012
20 x 20 x 1.5 cm
Glass, nylon, sterling silver; filled
COLLECTION OF THE PHILADELPHIA MUSEUM OF ART
PHOTOGRAPHY BY PAUL ROMANO

ANNA LOGINOVA
Still ■ 2012
75 x 3.5 x 3.5 cm
Momi paper, metallic thread; crocheted
PHOTOGRAPHY BY NICHOLAS KALIMIN

ROSA HIRN
Untitled ■ 2012
30 x 10 x 3 cm
Copper; sawn, bent, soldered
PHOTOGRAPHY BY ARTIST

JASMINE BOWDEN
A World without Bees ■ 2011
45 x 25 x 0.5 cm
Leather, adhesive; laser cut
PHOTOGRAPHY BY ARTIST

HANNA HEDMAN
While They Await Extinction ■ 2011
36 x 17 x 8 cm
Silver, copper, paint; fabricated, pierced,
soldered, oxidized, powder coated
PHOTOGRAPHY BY SANNA LINDBERG

SANDRA J. MATASICK
Heliotrope ■ 2011
Each pendant: 3 x 1.5 x 1.5 cm
South Sea pearl, freshwater pearls, 18-karat yellow gold,
Tahitian pearl, black spinel beads, 18-karat yellow gold;
hand carved, painted in wax, cast, hand constructed
PHOTOGRAPHY BY HAP SAKWA

Showcase 500
art necklaces

ERIN L. PRAIS-HINTZ
Winter into Spring ▣ 2012

20 x 1 x 1 cm
Ceramic bird, kyanite,
polymer clay; fold formed
PHOTOGRAPHY BY JOHN HARTMAN

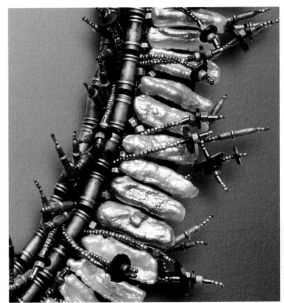

NADINE K. KARIYA
Dragon Pearl Bamboo Necklace ■ 2011
40.6 x 22.8 x 1.7 cm
Antique steel-cut beads, African brass beads,
vinyl wafers, fabric, monofilament; sewn, strung
PHOTOGRAPHY BY DANIEL FOX

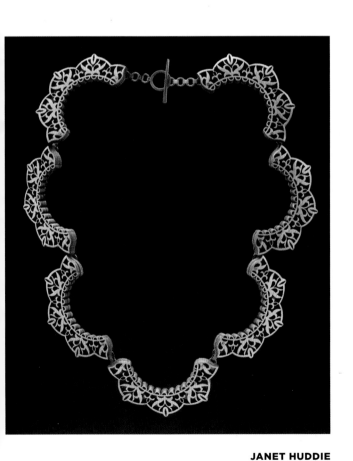

JANET HUDDIE
Sinan's Necklace ■ 2012
42 x 1.5 x 0.5 cm
Bamboo, sterling silver, gilder's wax,
patina; laser cut, hand fabricated
PHOTOGRAPHY BY JOSEPH HYDE

LIISA HASHIMOTO
Shoe Story Necklace ■ 2010
Pendant: 12 x 5 x 8 cm
Brass, silver
PHOTOGRAPHY BY TOSHIYUKI HATTORI

DAVINIA N. MIRAVAL
Copulace ■ 2010
30 x 2.5 x 2 cm
Papier-mâché, handmade paper,
polystyrene foam, magnets
PHOTOGRAPHY BY ARTIST

CLAIRE MCARDLE
Public Displays of Attention ■ 2011
60 x 50 x 12 cm
Silk; hand dyed, manipulated
PHOTOGRAPHY BY ARTIST

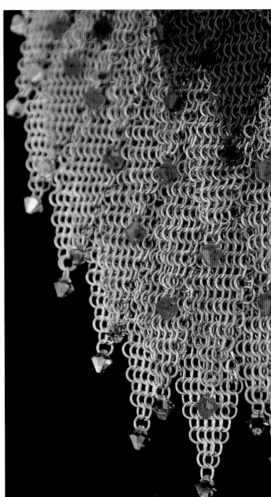

STEPHANIE CZAJA
Ring of Fire ■ 2012
23 x 18 cm
Anodized aluminum jump rings, Swarovski crystals,
copper clasp; European four-in-one chainmaille technique
PHOTOGRAPHY BY ARTIST

MARIAN ACOSTA CONTRERAS
Blossom Neckpiece ■ 2010

137 x 15 x 15 cm
Acrylic, canvas
PHOTOGRAPHY BY JINKYUN AHN

REBECCA WADE
Common Wax Flower ■ 2012

5.8 x 10.1 x 10.1 cm
Pigmented nylon, photopolymer; 3D printed
PHOTOGRAPHY BY ARTIST

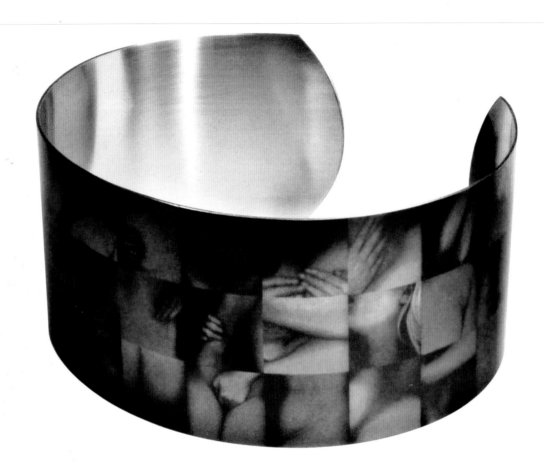

AGNIESZKA MAKSYMIUK
Intimacy Collar ■ 2011
14 x 11 x 6 cm
Sterling silver, stainless
steel; laser engraved
PHOTOGRAPHY BY ARTIST

JENNY BUTTERFIELD
Cascade Necklace ■ 2012
17 x 16 cm
Sterling silver, Brazilian agate;
etched, fabricated, set
BRAZILIAN AGATE BY JIM HARMAN
PHOTOGRAPHY BY ROBERT DIAMANTE

149

SHERRY H. SERAFINI
Monster ■ 2012
30.4 x 20.3 x 2.5 cm
Japanese seed beads, Swarovski crystal,
art glass, suede; bead embroidered
ART GLASS BY ANGI GRAHAM
PHOTOGRAPHY BY ARTIST

MARY LYNN PODILUK
Acrolect ■ 2012
30 x 30 x 4 cm
Gold-plated brass, dyed resin, bronze-wound steel wire, copper, magnets; cast, polished, stamped, fabricated, strung
PHOTOGRAPHY BY ARTIST

LINDA EDEIKEN
Ivory Reef ■ 2010
40.6 x 6.4 x 1.3 cm
Coral, moonstone, quartz, pearls, seed beads; freeform peyote stitch
PHOTOGRAPHY BY MELINDA HOLDEN

151

YONG JOO KIM
Reconfiguring the Ordinary: Twist Looped and Linked ■ 2011
57 x 40 x 10 cm
Hook-and-loop fasteners
PHOTOGRAPHY BY STUDIO MUNCH

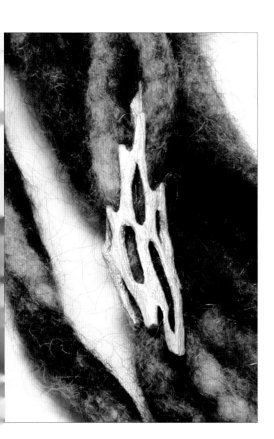

HILLAREY M. DEES
Opposite Attraction #1 ■ 2011
48.2 x 17.7 x 2.5 cm
Llama felt, sterling silver
PHOTOGRAPHY BY SUNG-YEOUL LEE

KATHERINE MORRIS
Quill Necklace ■ 2012
50 x 45 x 2.5 cm
Sterling silver, porcupine quills
PHOTOGRAPHY BY DAVID BUTLER

MICHAEL RYBICKI
PouredGrid:18 ■ 2011
20 x 20 x 1 cm
Sterling silver, brass, enamel, stainless
steel, copper; oxidized, etched
PHOTOGRAPHY BY ARTIST

EMILY EVERSGERD
Lunar Flare ■ 2010
40 x 20 x 3 cm
Fine silver, copper, rawhide; fabricated,
forged, fused, woven, oxidized
PHOTOGRAPHY BY MINDY HERRIN

WENDY ELLSWORTH
Wave Necklace ■ 2012

24.5 x 2 x 3 cm
Glass seed beads, lentils, daggers,
metal discs, Swarovski crystals,
freshwater pearls; gourd stitch
PHOTOGRAPHY BY DAVID ELLSWORTH

RACHEL NELSON-SMITH
PATTY LAKINSMITH
Dive ■ 2012
50.8 x 25.4 x 1 cm
Glass seed beads, nylon, silver; beadweaving

CESAR LIM
Amethyst Necklace ■ 2010
40.6 x 25.4 x 2.5 cm
Silver, gold, amethyst, citrines, aquamarines,
diamonds; forged, fabricated, oxidized
PHOTOGRAPHY BY VLAD LAVROVSKY

DARIA C. SALUS
Birds on a Wire Pendant ■ 2011
7.6 x 6.3 x 1.3 cm
Silver, copper, enamel; fabricated,
photo etched, embossed, bezel set

LAUREN ABRAMS
Lily ■ 2010
20.3 x 17.8 x 1.3 cm
Polymer clay, metal beads

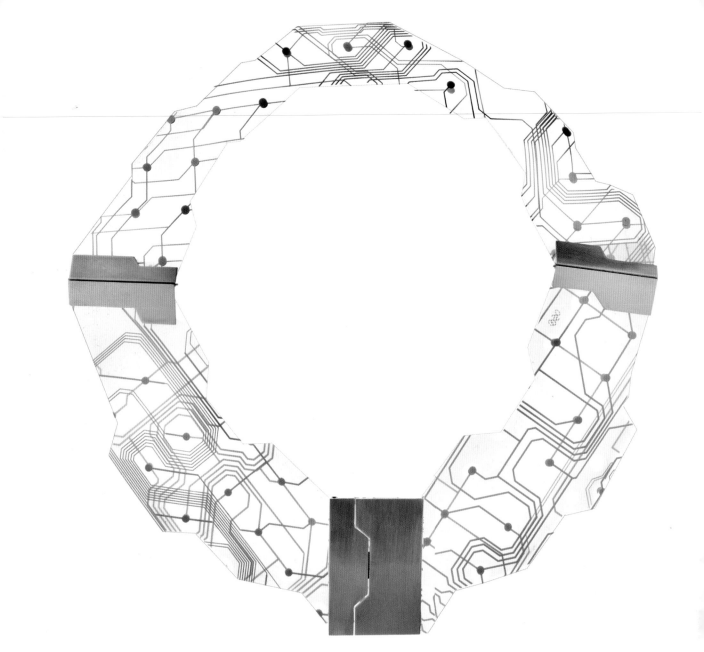

MARIA PIA PANZICA
Crossroads ■ 2011
20 x 20 x 2 cm
Silver, computer parts
PHOTOGRAPHY BY MARCELO MERLO

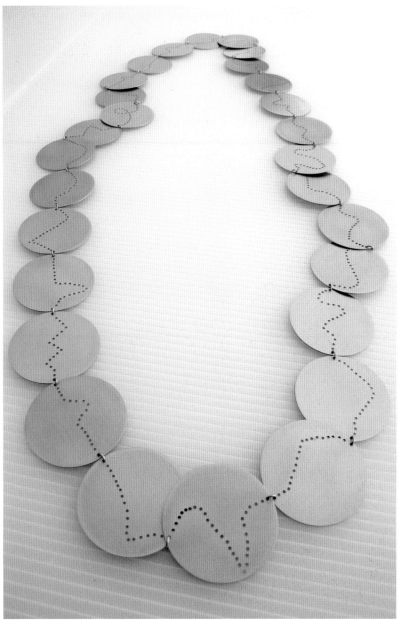

CHIAKI MIZUNO
28 Days ■ 2012
112 x 3.9 x 0.5 cm
Titanium
PHOTOGRAPHY BY ARTIST

161

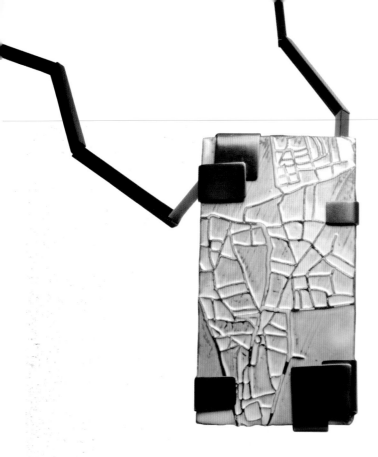

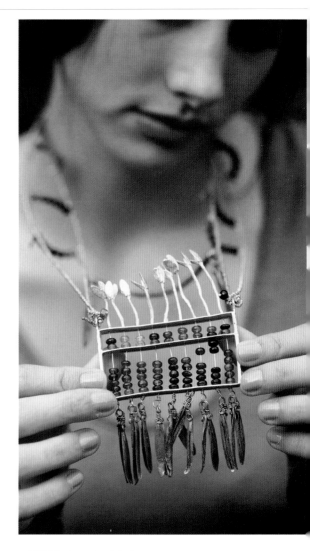

CRISTINA ZANI
From the Infinite Maps Series:
Madrid Necklace ■ 2012
45 x 5.5 x 0.6 cm
Copper, brass, enamel, nylon thread;
fabricated, photo etched, textured, oxidized
PHOTOGRAPHY BY ARTIST

KATHLEEN M. CARRICABURU
Tree of Knowledge ■ 2011
5 x 3.3 x 0.5 cm
Fine silver, sterling silver, green tourmaline
beads; fabricated, etched, cast
PHOTOGRAPHY BY JAYME KANANI

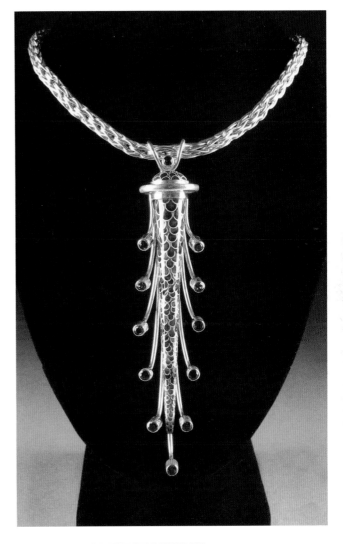

LISA KRÖBER
Untitled ■ 2012
35 x 25 x 13 cm
Silver, brass, black tourmaline
PHOTOGRAPHY BY ARTIST

SAMANTHA CORINNE MODERHOCK
Enamel Necklace ■ 2011
40 x 25 x 25 cm
Sterling silver, metal, enamel, sapphires;
hand crafted, fabricated, cast
PHOTOGRAPHY BY ARTIST

LIUDMYLA HEGGLAND
Peacock Flower ■ 2011
40 x 24 x 2 cm
Polymer clay, glass beads,
seed beads, cotton
PHOTOGRAPHY BY ARTIST

JANE MARTIN
About I Try ■ 2012
Overall length: 60 cm
Sterling silver, copper, nickel silver,
brass, bronze, jasper, agate, patina;
constructed, lacquered, married metal
PHOTOGRAPHY BY DOUGLAS YAPLE

165

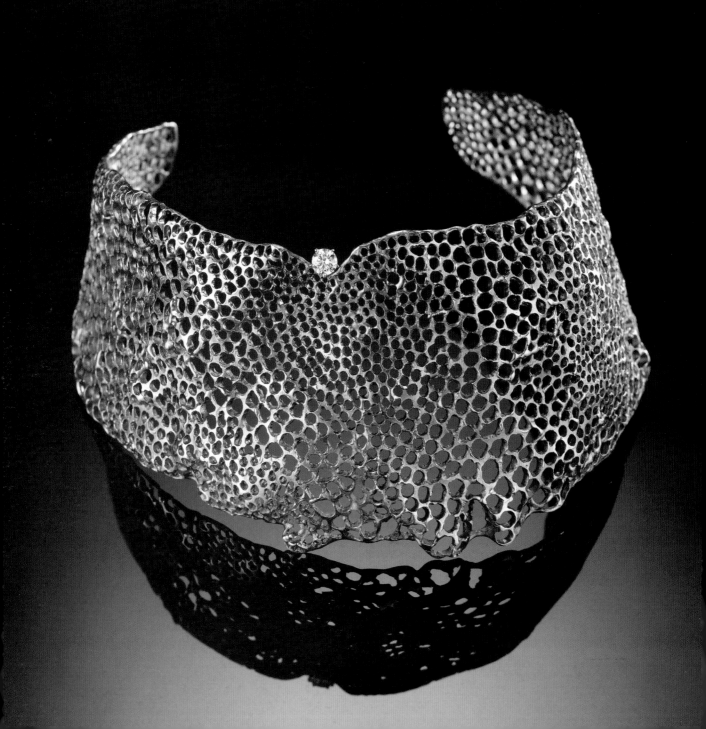

SATOKO NOBE
We See Hope ■ 2011
6.5 x 11 x 11 cm
Sterling silver, diamond; oxidized
PHOTOGRAPHY BY TOMOYA HARA

ROBERT EBENDORF
Sea Prince ■ 2010
24 x 4 x 0.5 cm
Mixed media
PHOTOGRAPHY BY STEVEN BRIAN SAMUELS

SARAH J. WALKER-HOLT
Untitled ■ 2011
34 x 15 x 3.5 cm
Domestic wooden implements, garden twine,
brass, silver, cotton, paper, pencil, wood putty
COURTESY OF THE FINGERS GALLERY
PHOTOGRAPHY BY MICHAEL COUPER

Showcase 500
art necklaces

THOMAS P. MUIR
Breath Diviner ■ 2011
Pendant: 16.5 x 5.7 x 2.5 cm
Brass, copper, silicone; formed,
fabricated, electroformed
PHOTOGRAPHY BY TIM THAYER

YAEL KRAKOWSKI
Black Coral Necklace ■ 2012
Pendant: 8.5 x 8.5 x 8.5 cm
Wool felt, glass beads, rubber;
sawed, crocheted
PHOTOGRAPHY BY ARTIST

HELEN SHIRK
Crimson Glory Necklace ■ 2011

23 x 23 x 1.5 cm
Sterling silver, china paint;
hand pierced, oxidized
PHOTOGRAPHY BY ARTIST

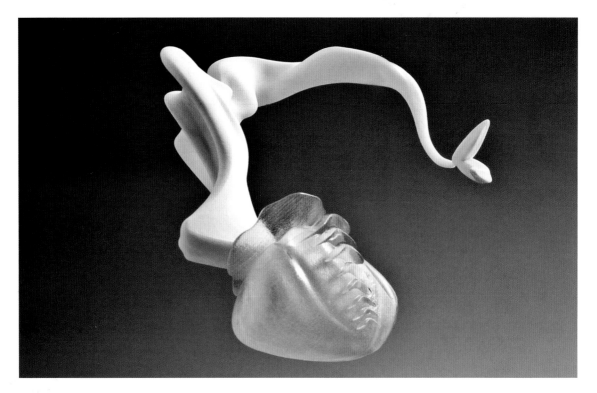

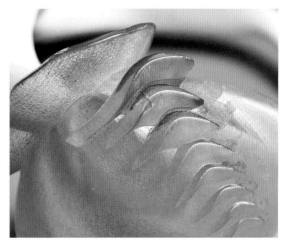

REBECCA WADE
Dutchman's Pipe ■ 2011
20.3 x 17.7 x 20.3 cm
Pigmented photopolymer,
pigmented nylon, 3D print
PHOTOGRAPHY BY ARTIST AND EMILY COBB

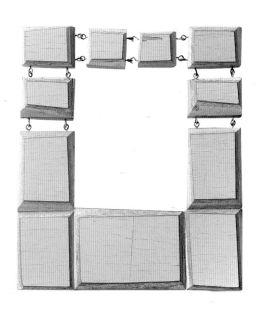

THEA CLARK
Roots ■ 2011
Pendant: 6.5 x 1.5 x 1.5 cm
Cyanotype on silk, wood, metal, found plastic,
tinted plastic, silver, cotton thread; oxidized
PHOTOGRAPHY BY STEVEN BRIAN SAMUELS

ANNA VAN DE POL DE DEUS
How Can I Say? ■ 2012
33.5 x 29 x 2.3 cm
Found wood, iron
PHOTOGRAPHY BY FEDERICO CAVICCHIOLI

173

LESLEY MESSAM
Clusters ■ 2011
Overall length: 81.2 cm
Sterling-silver metal clay, fine
silver, patina; lampworked,
soldered, torch fired, polished
PHOTOGRAPHY BY ABBY JOHNSON

JOSÈE DESJARDINS
Udaipur ■ 2010
50.8 x 30.4 x 20.3 cm
Sterling silver, 14-karat gold, old Indian
coins, plastic sheeting; constructed
PHOTOGRAPHY BY ANTHONY MCLEAN

I-HSUAN KUO
Tea-Time Role Play ■ 2011
13 x 7 x 0.8 cm
Copper, enamel, transfer paper
PHOTOGRAPHY BY ARTIST

LYNNE SUPROCK
Once upon a Time ■ 2012
3.8 x 3.2 x 1.3 cm
Patina, brass, copper, leather, stock paper;
book binding, image transfer, soldered
PHOTOGRAPHY BY ARTIST

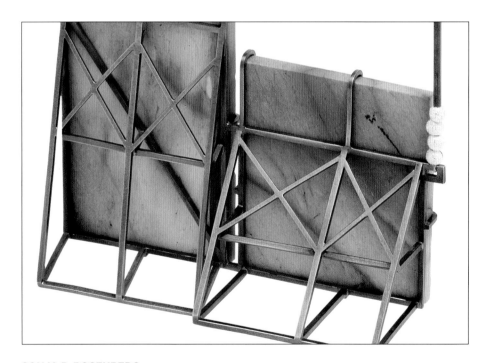

SONJA P. ROSENBERG
From the Erosion Series: Urban Decay 5 ■ 2012
Pendant: 7.7 x 9.5 x 3.5 cm
Sterling silver, mookaite, patina, silk thread
PHOTOGRAPHY BY ELIOT WRIGHT

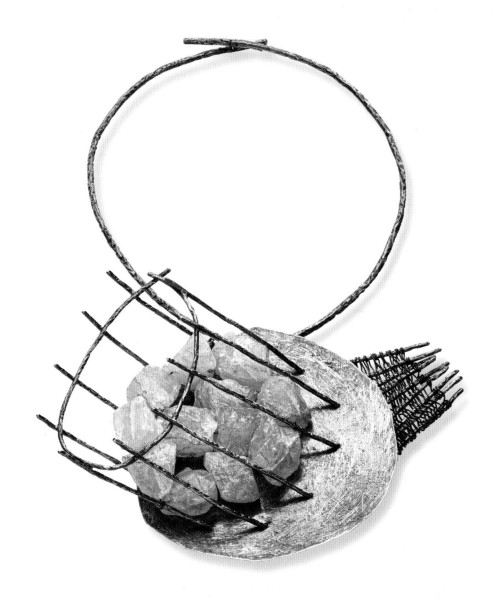

IRIS BODEMER
Untitled ■ 2012

28 x 18 x 4 cm
Silver, rose quartz, binding wire
PHOTOGRAPHY BY JULIAN KIRSCHLER

BECKY MEVERDEN
Maedeup Necklace ■ 2011
12 x 6 x 0.5 cm
Beads, cord; maedeup
(Korean knotting)
PHOTOGRAPHY BY CURTIS MEVERDEN

JOO YEON KIM
Mystery I ■ 2011
35 x 45 x 10 cm
Latex, Korean paper, aluminum
PHOTOGRAPHY BY MYOUNG-WOOK HUH

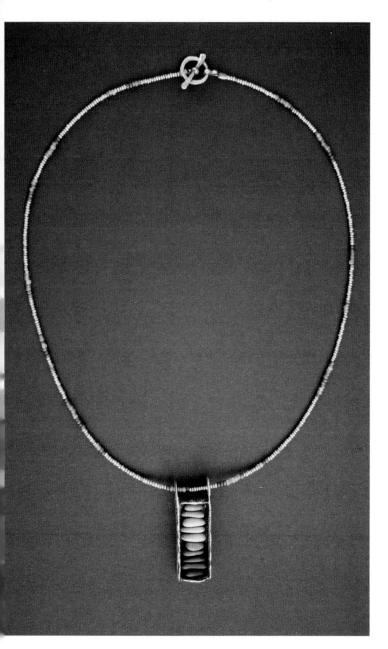

BIANCA EDMONDS
Heart Cairn ■ 2012
22 x 13 x 1.3 cm
Fine silver, Indonesian beach pebbles, sterling-silver wire,
antique and new seed beads, steel beading line, sterling-silver
clasp; hand fabricated, oxidized, drilled, riveted, strung
PHOTOGRAPHY BY ELISABETH EDWARDS

181

WILLIAM LLEWELLYN GRIFFITHS
Secret Locking Chamber Necklace ■ 2012

Pendant: 14.5 x 4.5 x 1.5 cm
18-karat yellow gold, 18-karat rose gold,
sterling silver, rose-cut white diamonds,
wood, silk; oxidized, lost wax cast
PHOTOGRAPHY BY ROBERT HART

GEORGE SAWYER

Fireflies' Garden ■ 2011

Pendant: 9.5 x 2 x 0.6 cm
14-karat palladium gray gold, patina, sterling silver, 18-karat yellow
gold, diamonds, natural hessonite garnet; diffusion bonded
STONE CUTTING BY TOM MUNSTEINER
PHOTOGRAPHY BY ALLEN BROWN

MARY DONALD
Red Boogie ■ 2012
38 x 2 x 2 cm
Plastic, silver; cut, formed, colored
PHOTOGRAPHY BY PATRICK LIOTTA

JACQUELINE RYAN
Neckpiece ■ 2011
65 x 1.6 x 1.6 cm
18-karat gold; hand pierced, forged
COURTESY OF THE SCOTTISH GALLERY, EDINBURGH. SCOTLAND
PHOTOGRAPHY BY ARTIST

RACHELLE THIEWES
Slipstream ■ 2012
38.1 x 34.3 x 12.7 cm
Steel, automobile paint
PHOTOGRAPHY BY ARTIST

ANTJE STOLZ
As Light as a Stone VIII ■ 2011
30 x 25 x 8 cm
Slate veneer, fluorescent enamel paint,
plastic, silk thread; sawed, cut
PHOTOGRAPHY BY PETRA MANDALKA

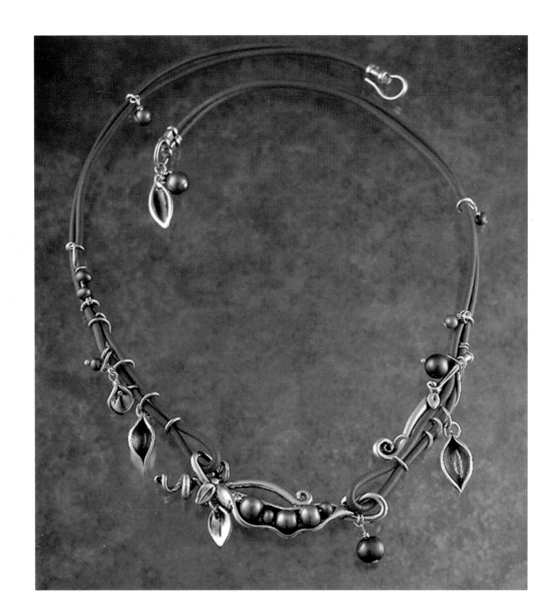

CAROLYN PHILLIPS
Pearls on a Vine ■ 2011
40.6 x 3 x 1.7 cm
Fine silver metal clay, freshwater pearls,
argentium silver wire, leather cord
PHOTOGRAPHY BY STEPHEN G. PHILLIPS

TISSA BERWANGER
Kronkorkenkette ■ 2010
66 x 5 x 5 cm
Silver, bottle caps
PHOTOGRAPHY BY ANDREAS DECKER

187

YONG JOO KIM
Reconfiguring the Ordinary:
Twist Looped and Attached ■ 2011
38 x 35 x 6 cm
Hook-and-loop fasteners, thread;
hand cut, assembled, and sewn
PHOTOGRAPHY BY STUDIO MUNCH

MARIAH TUTTLE
Abrupt Couture ■ 2011
45 x 50 x 6.5 cm
Caulk, paint, steel; handmade
PHOTOGRAPHY BY STEFFEN KNUDSEN ALLEN

MARIA PHILLIPS
Plaid Vest ■ 2012
44.5 x 25.4 x 5 cm
Wool vest; reconstructed
PHOTOGRAPHY BY ARTIST

ANDREW L. KUEBECK
Finally Coming Home ■ 2011
24 x 24 x 4 cm
Copper, sterling silver, enamel;
cast, fabricated, etched
PHOTOGRAPHY BY KEITH MEISER

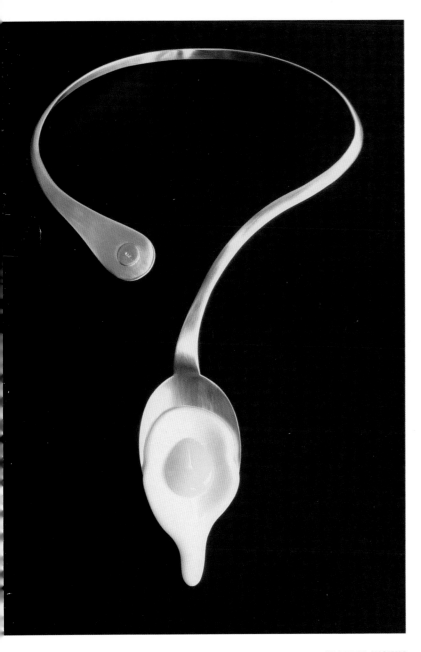

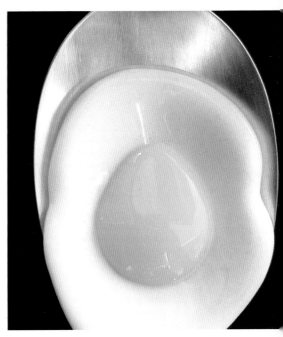

MARTY JESTIN
A Questionable Eggsample of a Yoke ■ 2012
24 x 14 x 5 cm
Acrylic, sterling silver, 18-karat
gold; hand forged, soldered
PHOTOGRAPHY BY ARTIST

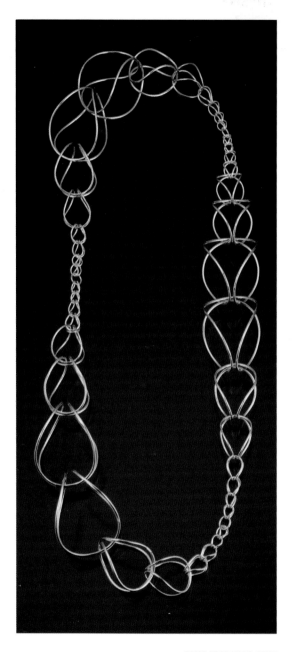

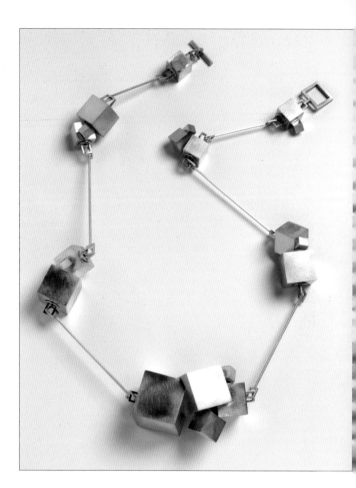

SUN KYOUNG KIM
Link 04 ■ 2012
71 x 3 x 3 cm
Sterling silver, fine
silver, 18-karat gold
PHOTOGRAPHY BY ARTIST

SUZAN REZAC
Untitled ■ 2012
56 x 3.8 x 3.1 cm
Sterling silver; constructed
PHOTOGRAPHY BY TOM VAN EYNDE

Showcase 500
art necklaces

JIM BOVÉ
Harvest Necklace ■ 2003
32 x 6 x 6 cm
Sterling silver, pill capsules; cast
PHOTOGRAPHY BY ARTIST

193

HSIA-MAN WANG
Bloom ■ 2012
50 x 4 x 3 cm
Sterling silver, agate, mica;
carved, fabricated, knitted
PHOTOGRAPHY BY ARTIST

Showcase 500
art necklaces

CARLY A. PETITT-TAYLOR
Cream Loop Necklace ■ 2010
50 x 7 x 0.4 cm
Vintage plastic, dental elastic,
rubber; heat fused
PHOTOGRAPHY BY AMANDA LITTLER PHOTOGRAPHY

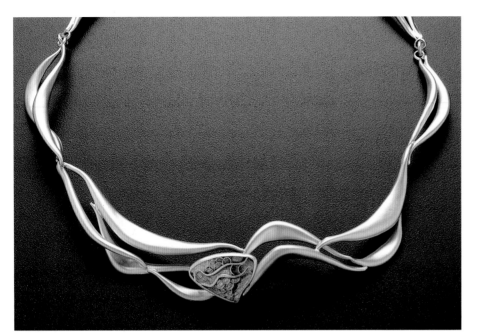

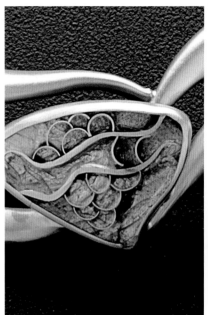

MICHAEL BANNER
MAUREEN BANNER
Neck Vines and Cloisonné Collar ■ 2012
28 x 28 x 2.5 cm
Enamel, sterling-silver sheet; high-fired cloisonné, mounted
in anticlastic, shell formed, fabricated, constructed
PHOTOGRAPHY BY JOHN POLAK

CAROLYN A. YOUNG
Tundra Swans Necklace ■ 2011
14 x 15 x 1.5 cm
Sterling silver, mulberry paper, acrylic,
nylon-coated sterling silver cable; hand
fabricated, soldered, hammered, formed
PHOTOGRAPHY BY ARTIST

EVAN LARSON-VOLTZ
Inversion ■ 2012
48.2 x 40.6 x 8.8 cm
Copper, brass, paper, wood; fold formed,
slot-and-tab construction
PHOTOGRAPHY BY ARTIST

RAHEL PFROMMER
Body Piece ■ 2012
38 x 30 x 15 cm
Nylon, brass; woven, blackened
PHOTOGRAPHY BY CHRISTIAN METZLER

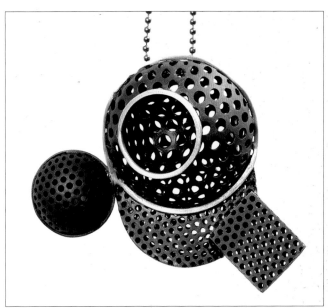

JIN AH JO
Home and Away ■ 2011
Home (left): 8 x 8 x 1.5 cm
Away (right): 8 x 4.5 x 3.5 cm
Mild steel, silver; sand
blasted, forged, soldered
PHOTOGRAPHY BY SOTHA BOURN

SUSAN MATYCH-HAGER
Memories of Autumns Past ■ 2012

30.5 x 25.5 x 6.5 cm
Glass beads made by the artist, copper
wire, Swarovski crystals; flameworked
PHOTOGRAPHY BY JERRY ANTHONY

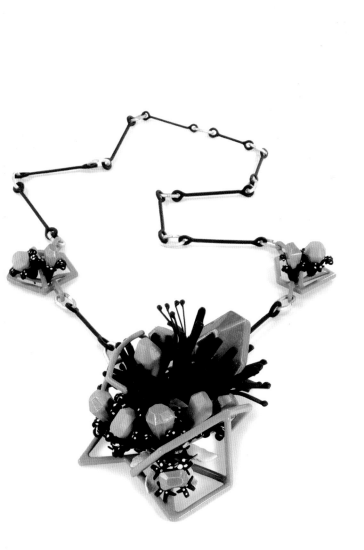

MICHAEL DALE BERNARD

From the Irregular Cuts Series: Pale Blue Frost Necklace ■ 2012

46 x 20 x 5 cm

Recycled copper and steel, reclaimed wood, sterling silver, stainless steel, lacquer; fabricated, fused, welded, powder coated, carved, spray painted

PHOTOGRAPHY BY ARTIST

DENISE J. REYTAN

Verreauxxi ■ 2010

26 x 14 x 2.5 cm

Carnelian, coral, rose quartz, smoky quartz, garnet, silver, stainless steel, silicone, plastic, resin, rope; cast

PHOTOGRAPHY BY M. FISCHINGER

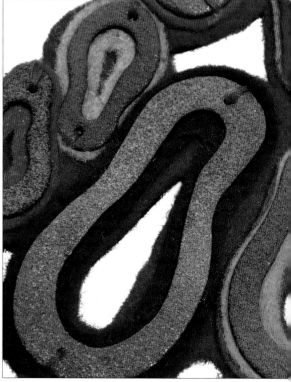

LAURA A. RUSSO
Footsteps ■ 2012

35 x 20 x 0.4 cm
Copper, enamel, handmade felt,
cotton thread, leather; textured
PHOTOGRAPHY BY DAMIÁN WASSER

TRACY L. BLACK
Picnic Corsage Choker ■ 2012
5.1 x 50.8 x 3.8 cm
Vinyl tablecloth, copper,
silver, resin, thread
PHOTOGRAPHY BY ARTIST

LINDA RETTICH
Kente Reversible Collar ■ 2012
27.9 x 27.9 x 1.3 cm
Seed beads; needle
woven, manipulated
PHOTOGRAPHY BY DAVID KATZ

JOHN WIK
Spector ■ 2011
Overall length: 40 cm
Anodized aluminum, die-cast
section from a toy car; chainmail
PHOTOGRAPHY BY ARTIST

MELISSA INGRAM
Arabesque Armor ■ 2012
37 x 21 x 1.5 cm
Seed beads, berry beads, Swarovski crystal chatons, pearls,
bicones, rounds, chessboard, and rivoli beads, rocailles, upcycled
necklace pendants and beads, tubing, wire, enameled chain

TANJA ROOLFS
Flower Necklace ■ 2012
100 x 6 x 6 cm
Sterling silver, olivine, agate
PHOTOGRAPHY BY HERMANN RECKNAGEL

BARBARA SMITH MCLAUGHLIN
Pieces of Love ■ 2012
Overall length: 53.3 cm
Sterling silver, reticulated silver, bronze, onyx, brookite,
citrine, jasper, tourmaline; fabricated, fused, linked
GEMSTONES CUT BY THE LATE ROBERT MERRILL, ROBERT D. MCLAUGHLIN, 3R., AND MICHAEL DYBER
PHOTOGRAPHY BY HAP SAKWA

BARBARA POOLE
Necklace Seed Series Side ■ 2012
51 x 5 x 5 cm
Merino wool, glass beads,
Swarovski crystals, stainless
steel; wet and needle felted
PHOTOGRAPHY BY CLEMENTS & HOWCRAFT

KATHLEEN NOWAK TUCCI
Naida Necklace ■ 2011
22 x 10 x 2 cm
Recycled bicycle inner
tubes; die cut
PHOTOGRAPHY BY ROBERT DIAMANTE

Showcase 500
art necklaces

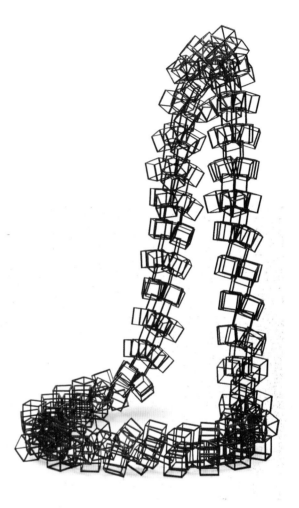

HELEN SHIRK
Hematite Trace Necklace ■ 2010
27.5 x 23 x 0.5 cm
Sterling silver; hand pierced, oxidized
PHOTOGRAPHY BY ARTIST

BIN DIXON-WARD
Framework ■ 2012
35 x 35 x 4 cm
Nylon, ink; CAD drawn,
3D printed, hand colored
PHOTOGRAPHY BY JEREMY DILLON

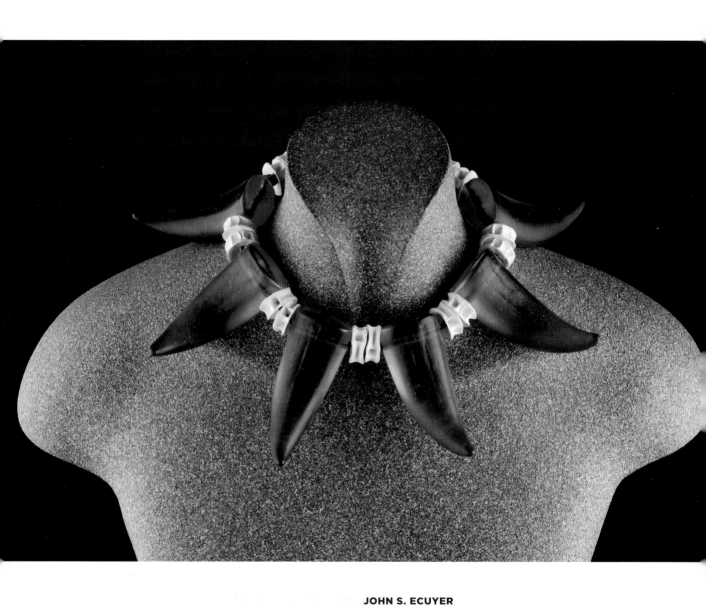

JOHN S. ECUYER
Antipodean Neckpiece ■ 2012
27 x 27 x 4 cm
Shark vertebrae, glass,
cord; kiln fired, cast
PHOTOGRAPHY BY ARTIST

LINDA KINDLER-PRIEST
Oil on Water ■ 2011

17.7 x 17.7 cm
Charoite stones, ruby, silver,
14-karat gold; hand cut,
sculpted, oxidized, repoussé
PHOTOGRAPHY BY GORDON BERNSTEIN

211

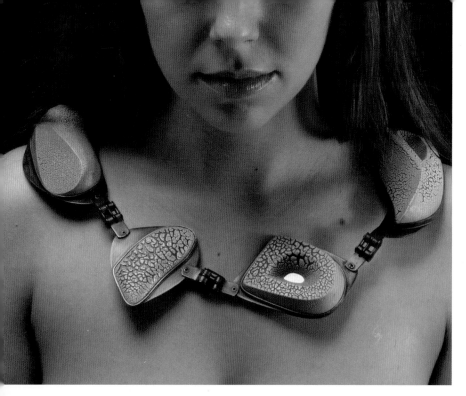

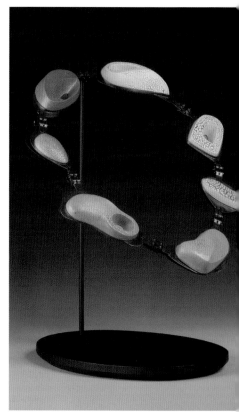

JOHN-THOMAS L. RICHARD
Grand Canyon National Park Necklace ■ 2010

30 x 29.2 x 2.5 cm
Slip-cast ceramic, copper, crackle
glaze; textured, etched
PHOTOGRAPHY BY ROBLY GLOVER

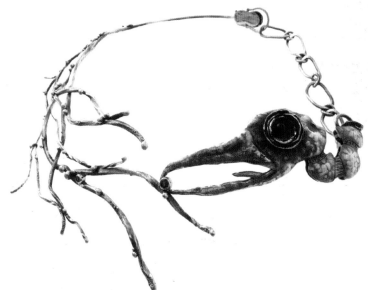

VONNA L. MASLANKA
Storm ■ 2010

Overall length: 43.2 cm
Vintage and new brass findings, chain,
old earring parts, seed beads, buttons,
pearls; strung, free-form peyote stitch
PHOTOGRAPHY BY ARTIST

AUDREY BOUDREAULT
À la Vie, à la Mort (Of Life and Death) ■ 2010

55 x 23 x 22 cm
Sterling silver, 18-karat yellow gold, garnets,
onyx; repoussé, chased, fabricated, fused
PHOTOGRAPHY BY ISABELLE MÉTIVIER

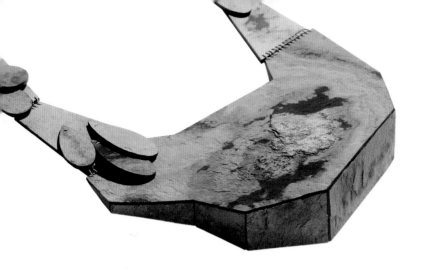
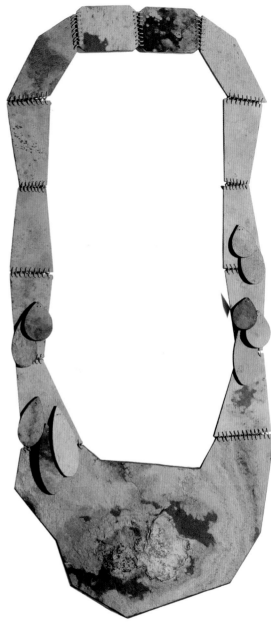

ANTJE STOLZ
I Am a Rock ■ 2012
45 x 20 x 5 cm
Slate veneer, polyurethane, enamel paint,
silk thread, lead; hollow mounted, sewed
PHOTOGRAPHY BY PETRA MANDALKA

GIANCARLO MONTEBELLO
Superleggeri Tondo ■ 2007
23 x 2 cm
Stainless steel, resin, 18-karat gold;
laquered, chemical cut process
PHOTOGRAPHY BY ARNALDO GENITRINI

CHRISTINE H. MACKELLAR
Garland Necklace ■ 2011
Overall length: 45 cm
Sterling silver, 18-karat gold, graduated
rutilated quartz; textured, fabricated
PHOTOGRAPHY BY HAP SAKWA

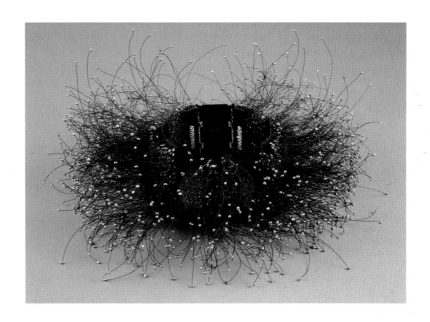

KAREN BACHMANN
Burnt Cube Necklace ■ 2012

48 x 4.5 x 4.5 cm
Maple, volcanic stone, sterling silver;
hand carved, pyrography, strung
PHOTOGRAPHY BY RALPH GABRINER

CAROL SALISBURY
Iron Necklace #1 ■ 2011

35.6 x 35.6 x 8.9 cm
Iron binding wire, brass, brazing
rod; woven, fabricated, etched
PHOTOGRAPHY BY ARTIST

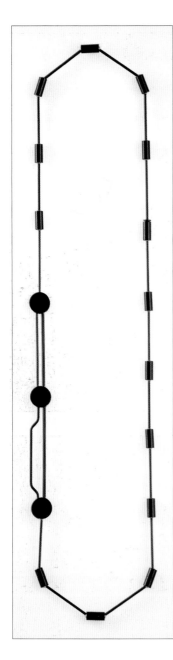

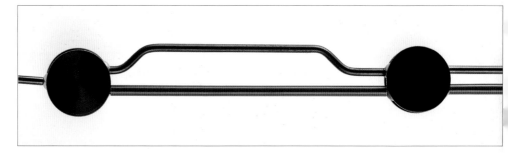

PHOEBE PORTER
Transit Necklace ■ 2012

44 x 10 x 1 cm
Titanium, aluminum, stainless steel;
machined, anodized, assembled
PHOTOGRAPHY BY ANDREW SIKORSKI

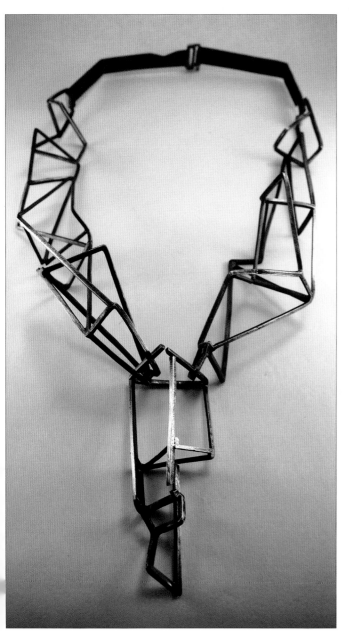

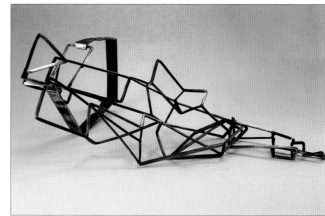

DINA GONZALEZ MASCARO
Invisible Stones ◼ 2011

36 x 18 x 5 cm
Sterling silver; hand built,
soldered, textured, oxidized
PHOTOGRAPHY BY ARTIST

219

ANDREA CODERCH VALOR
Untitled ■ 2010

3 x 10 x 2 cm
Silver, pearls, plastic
PHOTOGRAPHY BY FEDERICO CAVICCHIOLI

MARCUS I. SYNNOT
Splendid Blue Wren ■ 2012

7.4 x 10.6 x 1.5 cm
Fine silver, enamel; torch fired
PHOTOGRAPHY BY MATT REED

KIM YEOJIN
Doubtful Relation ■ 2010
Pendant: 13 x 13 x 5 cm
Glass, nickel, polymer clay
PHOTOGRAPHY BY ARTIST

ASHLEY BUCHANAN
Selective Piercing Neckpiece ■ 2012
30 x 14 cm
Brass, charcoal; hand pierced,
powder coated
PHOTOGRAPHY BY ARTIST

LAWRENCE WOODFORD
Sacred Stone Sacred Geometry ■ 2011
Overall length: 55.8 cm
Silver, earthenware, topaz, wood,
gold leaf, paint, recycled glass
PHOTOGRAPHY BY ANTHONY MCLEAN

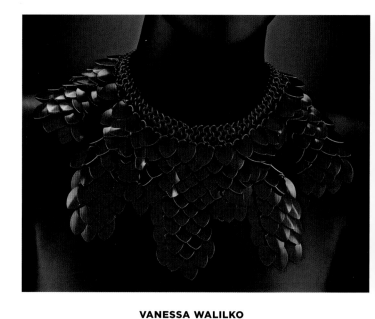

YENHWA LU
Fortune Bag ■ 2012
30 x 30 x 5 cm
Copper mesh, calabash,
cotton thread; linked
PHOTOGRAPHY BY JO LU

VANESSA WALILKO
Red Queen ■ 2010
26 x 26 x 1 cm
Aluminum; die cut,
anodized, cold connected
PHOTOGRAPHY BY LARRY SANDERS

Showcase 500
art necklaces

KATIE SCHUTTE
Sabellida Motif Collar ■ 2010

10.1 x 40.6 x 35.5 cm
Found wire; crocheted,
powder coated
PHOTOGRAPHY BY JEFF SABO

ALEJANDRA SOLAR
Untitled ■ 2011
Pendant: 7 x 4 x 3 cm
Photo transfer in polyurethane,
nylon string
PHOTOGRAPHY BY ARTIST

FACING PAGE
JILLIAN MATTHEWS
Suspension Necklace ■ 2012
33 x 16.5 x 7.6 cm
Mahogany, epoxy, brass; oxidized
PHOTOGRAPHY BY DENISE LEBREUX

ELIZABETH A. LYNE
For Helen ■ 2011
30.5 x 25.4 x 0.8 cm
Fine silver, sterling silver, dyed freshwater
pearls, sapphire; hand woven, fabricated
PHOTOGRAPHY BY JASON DOWDLE

LISA KRÖBER
Untitled ■ 2012
27 x 13 x 1 cm
Silver, ebony, black tourmaline
PHOTOGRAPHY BY ARTIST

Showcase 500
art necklaces

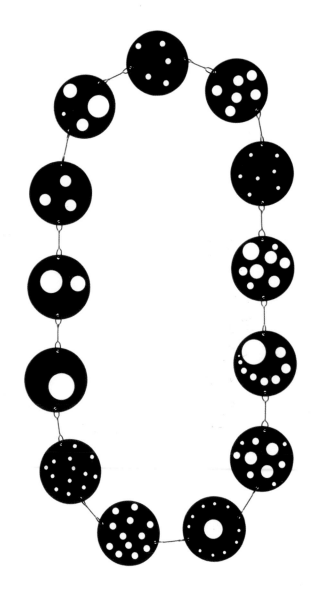

JACQUELINE L. CULLEN
Hand-Carved Whitby Jet Pendant with
Electro-Formed Precious Metal ■ 2011
100 x 10 x 0.7 cm
Whitby jet, fine silver, 18-karat gold heavy vermeil,
18-karat gold, silk; hand carved, hand built
PHOTOGRAPHY BY SUSSIE AHLBURG

TORE SVENSSON
Thirteen ■ 2011
28 x 14 x 5 cm
Steel, linseed oil; etched,
soldered, fired
PHOTOGRAPHY BY FRANZ KARL

229

ANDREW COSTEN
Aqua and Ice ■ 2011
51.2 x 30.6 x 9.4 cm
19-karat white gold, fancy-cut
aquamarine, brilliant-cut diamonds
PHOTOGRAPHY BY SARAH-HANNAH BEDARD

LEILA TAI
Clip-On Leaves Drop ■ 2011
5.8 x 2.5 x 0.7 cm
18-karat gold, diamond accent; plique-à-jour
PHOTOGRAPHY BY RALPH GABRINER

VALERIE BROWN
Tidal Pool Necklace ■ 2011
24 x 5.5 x 1 cm
Enamel, fine silver, sterling silver, 18-karat
yellow gold, baroque pearl, freshwater pearls;
cloisonné, fabricated, cast, hand knotted

RENEE DAVIS
Mers ■ 2012
Pendant: 7.6 x 3.8 x 1.2 cm
Argentium sterling silver, turquoise,
freshwater pearls, ammonite;
hand fabricated, etched

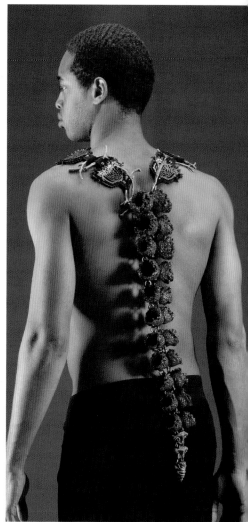

REBECCA A. BEALS
Vivere Spina (Living Spine) ■ 2012
30 x 14 x 2 cm
Found objects, leather, copper, bronze,
paint, acrylic medium, thread, carnelian,
patina; assembled, cast, laser cut
PHOTOGRAPHY BY ROBLY A. GLOVER

Showcase 500
art necklaces

MENGNAN QU
Blind Men Touch Elephant ■ 2012

16 x 12 x 1 cm
Copper, fine silver, sterling silver,
enamel, coral, thread; cloisonné
PHOTOGRAPHY BY YU XIA

233

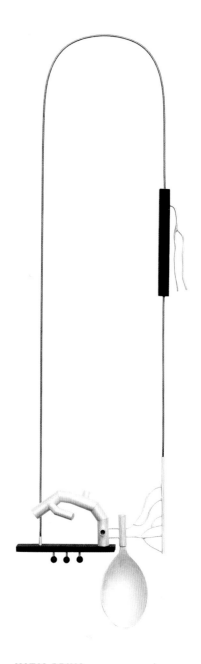

HEATHER RATHBUN
Adjustable Necklace with Puzzle Clasp ■ 2011
Pendant: 5.6 x 7.6 x 0.9 cm
Sterling silver, roller chain;
fabricated, cast
PHOTOGRAPHY BY ARTIST

KATJA PRINS
*Inter-Act Necklace *1* ■ 2011
55 x 10 x 2 cm
Silver, reconstructed
onyx, steel wire
PHOTOGRAPHY BY HAROLD STRAK

Showcase 500
art necklaces

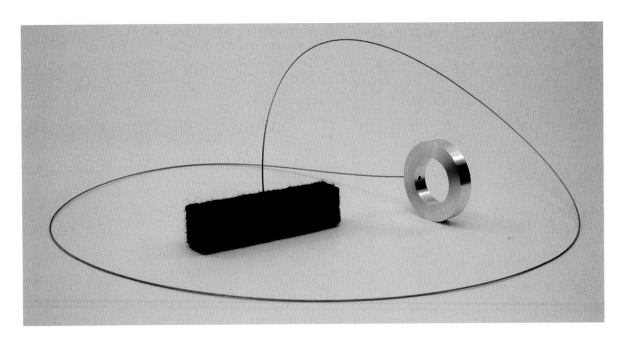

JENS CLAUSEN
Close ■ 2012
65 x 15 x 15 cm
Sterling silver, wool, stainless
steel wire, bronze; fabricated,
felted, dyed, assembled
PHOTOGRAPHY BY ARTIST

CATHERINE A. BUCKLEY
Highland Fling Necklace ■ 2011
Centerpiece: 6 cm
Overall length: 45.7 cm
Sari ribbon, brass, silver plate,
copper, alcohol inks, glass; filigree
PHOTOGRAPHY BY ARTIST

AMANDA J. FRAZIER
Theodora ■ 2011
25.4 x 20.3 x 2.5 cm
Bronze, butterflies,
resin; forged, cast
PHOTOGRAPHY BY ARTIST

Showcase 500
art necklaces

KVETOSLAVA FLORA SEKANOVA
Untitled ■ 2012
Pendant: 10.5 x 9 cm
Newsprint, acrylic paint, silver, adhesive,
silk thread, mixed media; laminated, carved,
layered, hollowed, reconstructed, manipulated
PHOTOGRAPHY BY JAROSLAV POLONY

ANDREA ARIAS
Paseando por el Barrio ■ 2011

10 x 8 cm
Colored pencils, resin, silver
PHOTOGRAPHY BY FEDERICO CAVICHIOLLI

239

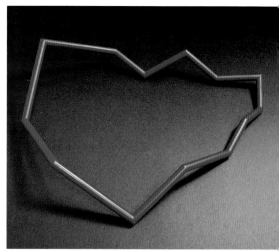
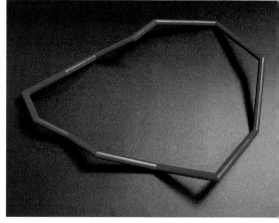

YU HIRAISHI
Untitled ■ 2012
30.5 x 24 x 4.3 cm
Brass pipe, paint; soldered
PHOTOGRAPHY BY ARTIST

CATALINA BRENES
Petunia ■ 2010
27 x 12 x 2 cm
Brass, fabric, silk thread;
hand stitched, welded
PHOTOGRAPHY BY FEDERICO CAVICCHIOLI

SARA BROWN
A Place, No Place ■ 2011
42 x 14 x 2.5 cm
Copper, enamel; electroformed,
torch fired, fabricated, oxidized
PHOTOGRAPHY BY ARTIST

DIANE D. DENNIS
Star Light Star Bright ■ 2012
58.5 x 16 x 1 cm
Seed beads, Swarovski crystal rounds;
peyote stitch, Ndebele/herringbone stitch
PHOTOGRAPHY BY ARTIST

EDGAR A. LOPEZ
Caribbean Dream ◾ 2012

24.1 x 11.4 cm
Larimar stones, crystals, turquoise,
24-karat gold seed beads
PHOTOGRAPHY BY GIOVANNI CAVALLARO

AMY JOHNSON
Sunset Blossoms ■ 2011
50.8 x 10 x 3 cm
Crystals, cabochons, glass pearls,
seed beads; right-angle weave
PHOTOGRAPHY BY LARRY SANDERS

KATHLEEN CAID
Wings of Joy ■ 2011

Butterfly: 10 x 12 x 1 cm
New and vintage glass and crystal beads,
shell cabochons, rhinestones, jasper,
aquamarine; bead embroidered
PHOTOGRAPHY BY BERNARD WOLF

LAURA J. MCCABE
Antique Yellow Glass-Spiked Choker ■ 2012

2.5 x 5 x 35.5 cm
Custom-cut antique yellow glass spikes, glass seed
beads, freshwater pearls, crystal beads, 14-karat
gold clasp; peyote stitch, herringbone stitch
PHOTOGRAPHY BY MELINDA HOLDEN

W. JOHN MACMULLEN
Woman of Letters ■ 2012
55 x 5 x 5 cm
Computer keyboard keys,
metal chain, metal rings
PHOTOGRAPHY BY ARTIST

ROBLY A. GLOVER
Yellow Bobber Necklace ■ 2011
60 x 60 cm
Sterling silver, found
objects; cold connected
PHOTOGRAPHY BY ARTIST

247

ELKA FRELLER
Rock in Pearls ■ 2011
40 x 15 x 3 cm
Leather, sterling silver, pearls
PHOTOGRAPHY BY JOSE TERRA NOGUEIRA

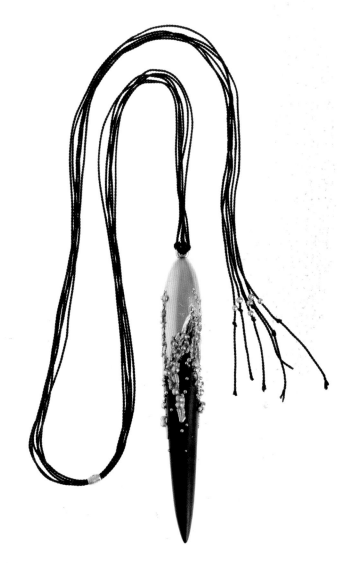

JUNHEE BAE
Rain ▪ 2011
48.7 x 8.8 x 1.7 cm
Sterling silver, rice paper,
Chinese ink, resin
PHOTOGRAPHY BY MYUNG-WOOK HUH

JACQUELINE L. CULLEN
Whitby Jet Pendant ▪ 2012
13 x 0.6 x 0.6 cm
Whitby jet, fine silver, 18-karat gold
vermeil, 18-karat gold, silk
PHOTOGRAPHY BY SUSSIE AHLBURG

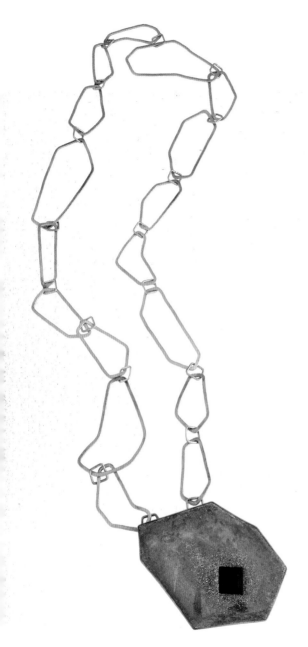

EMMA L. BUGG ■ 2012
Observatory Necklace
96 x 8 x 0.4 cm
24-karat gold plate, gold dust, Tasmanian black spinel,
concrete, Triassic age sandstone from the Museum of
Old and New Art, Hobart, Tasmania, Australia
PHOTOGRAPHY BY ARTIST

JUDITH KAUFMAN
Walk in the Woods ■ 2010

14 x 2 cm
Amber, 22-karat gold,
diamonds; fabricated
PHOTOGRAPHY BY TONY PETTINATO

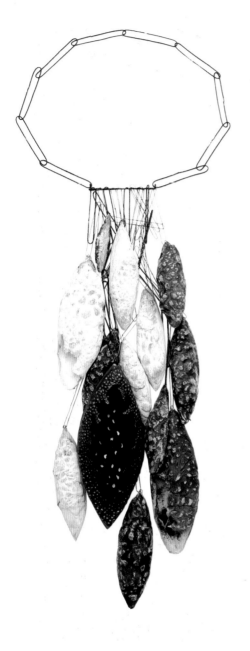

TAMMY YOUNG EUN KIM
Untitled ■ 2012
55.8 x 22.8 x 12.7 cm
Handmade paper, steel,
copper; chased, repoussé
PHOTOGRAPHY BY SETH PAPAC

KATHRYN M. OSGOOD
Ocean ■ 2011
Pendant: 9 x 7 x 2 cm
Copper, enamel, sterling
silver; fabricated
PHOTOGRAPHY BY ROBERT DIAMANTE

Showcase 500
art necklaces

LIA TAJCNAR
Ceremonial Chaos ■ 2012
45 x 30 x 2.5 cm
Porcelain, resin,
mixed media
PHOTOGRAPHY BY ARTIST

253

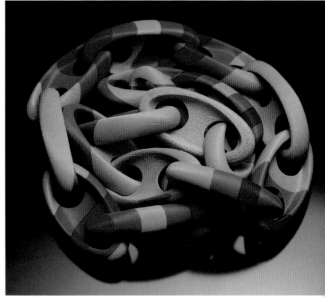
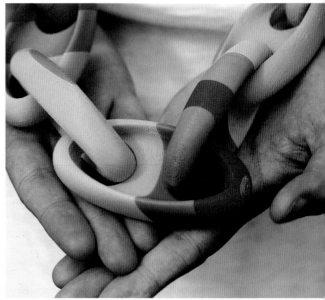

REBECCA STRZELEC
...all things nice ■ 2012
43.1 x 8.8 x 4.5 cm
Plastic; CAD, rapid prototype
PHOTOGRAPHY BY ADAM VORLICEK

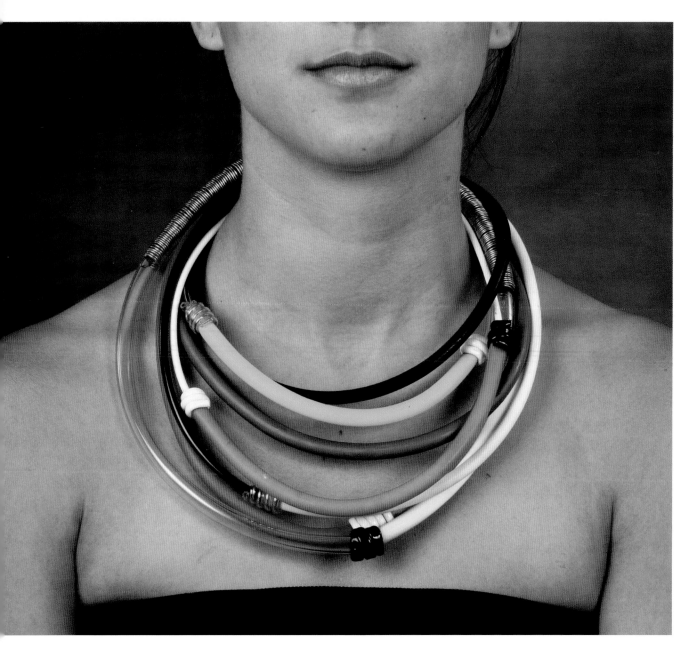

GABRIELLE N. MORRIS
Masai Mara ■ 2011
25.4 x 20.3 x 2.5 cm
Rubber, latex, brass wire
PHOTOGRAPHY BY MAUREEN VACCARO

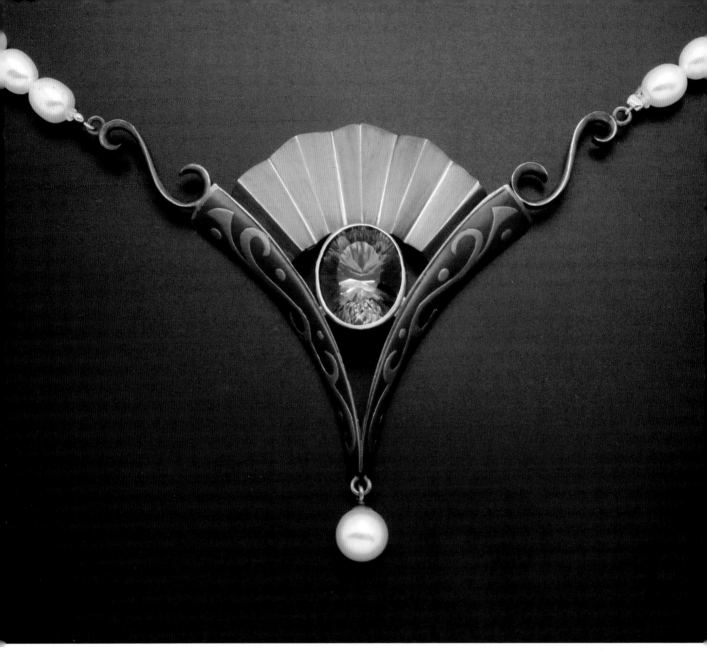

STEVEN KOLODNY
Eternal Sea Life ■ 2012

8.1 x 2.5 cm
18-karat gold, silver, ammonite fossil, diamond,
South Sea pearl; oxidized, hammer raised,
hollow constructed, micro-granulation
PHOTOGRAPHY BY RALPH GABRINER

SUZANNE EVON
Black Plumb Bob Treasure ■ 2010

50.8 x 0.7 x 0.7 cm
Sterling silver, 18-karat gold vermeil;
oxidized, fabricated, cast
PHOTOGRAPHY BY HAP SAKWA

257

MARGOT DI CONO
Spider ■ 2011
22.8 x 20.3 x 2.5 cm
18-karat gold, 24-karat
gold, sterling silver
PHOTOGRAPHY BY ARTIST

HYE YOON PARK
Dream ■ 2011
27 x 21 x 4 cm
Bronze, copper wire, sterling-silver
wire; 24-karat gold plated
PHOTOGRAPHY BY ARTIST

259

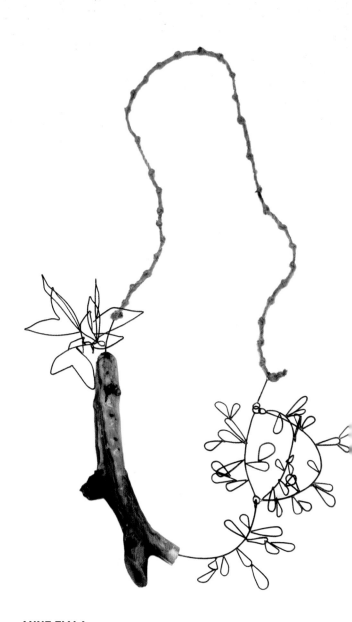

TIMOTHY M. MCMAHON
Helvenka ■ 2012
24 x 12 x 1.5 cm
Black palm, steel, brass;
powder coated
PHOTOGRAPHY BY ARTIST

ANNE FIALA
Keeping My Regrets ■ 2011
49.5 x 22.8 x 6.3 cm
Wood, steel, twine, paint; fabricated
PHOTOGRAPHY BY ARTIST

LINDSAY WISECUP
Season of Fire and Night ■ 2010

56 x 5 cm
Nickel silver, copper, brass, steel, turquoise,
Czech glass, Japanese seed beads, raw linen;
fabricated, etched, textured, oxidized
PHOTOGRAPHY BY ARTIST

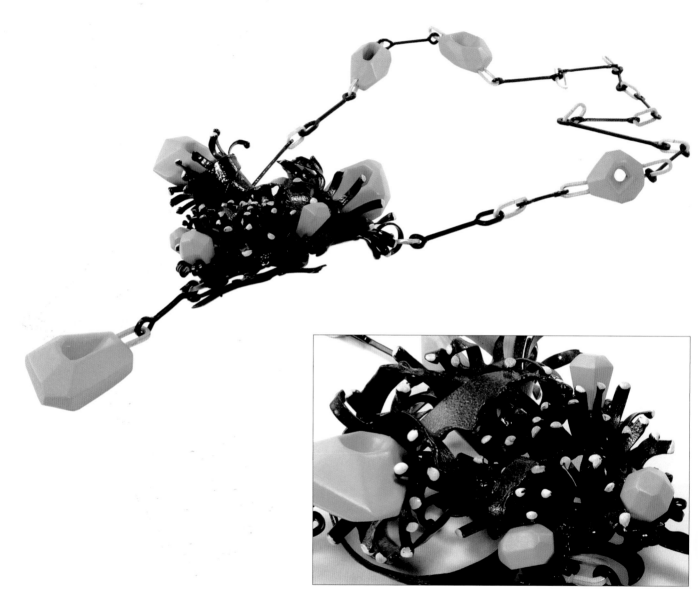

MICHAEL DALE BERNARD
From the Irregular Cut Series: Moss Vein Tiffany Necklace ■ 2012
55 x 20 x 8 cm
Recycled steel and copper, reclaimed wood, sterling
silver, stainless steel, spray paint, lacquer; fused,
welded, fabricated, carved, powder coated
PHOTOGRAPHY BY ARTIST

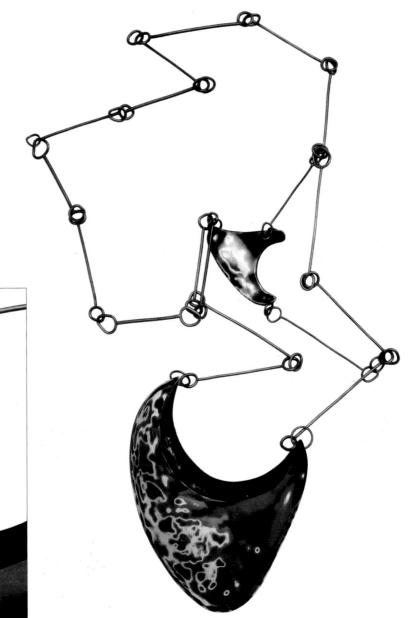

RENE L. HENRY
Colorform ■ 2012
55 x 12.5 x 5 cm
Copper, spray paint; die formed,
fabricated, textured, anticlastic raising,
wire construction, sanded, oxidized
PHOTOGRAPHY BY SETH PAPAC

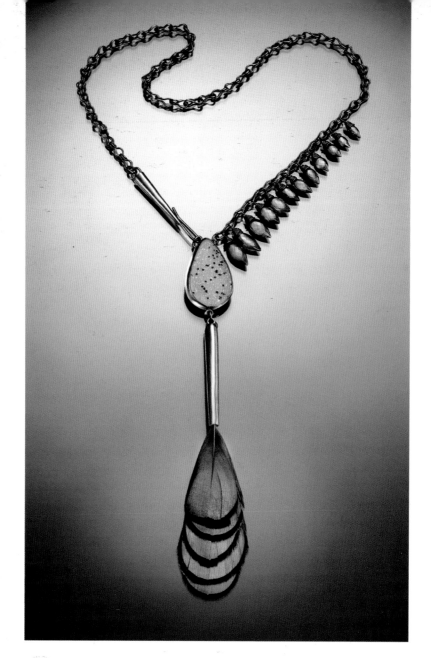

WINNIE CHAI
Presence #2 ■ 2012

33 x 2.5 x 1.3 cm
Sterling silver, fine silver, druzy,
gemstones, pheasant feathers,
patina; fabricated, fused, formed

FACING PAGE
MEGAN N. CLARK
Stingray Feather Necklace ■ 2012

44 x 4 x 0.3 cm
Sterling silver, 18-karat yellow gold,
yellow sapphires, leather; hand formed
and fabricated, bezel set, inlaid

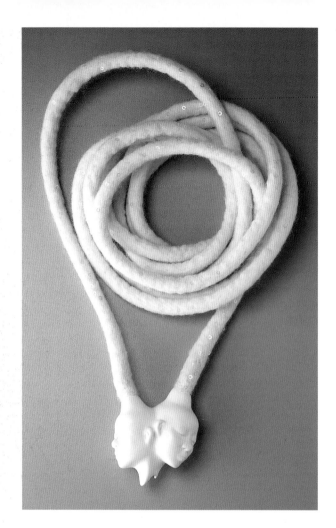

HYEWON KIM
Love ■ 2011
25.4 x 10.1 x 11.4 cm
Resin; cast
PHOTOGRAPHY BY MYUNG-WOOK HUH

MOMOKO KUMAI
Paper Necklace ■ 2011
40 x 20 x 4 cm
Paper; folded, twisted, rolled
PHOTOGRAPHY BY ARTIST

Showcase **500**
art necklaces

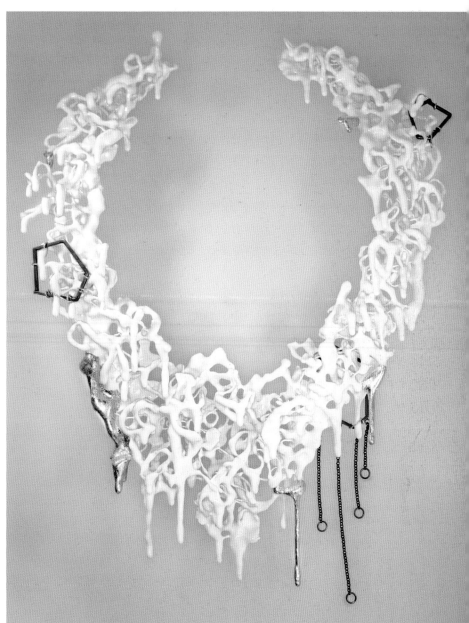

KAROLINA BIK
Chaos Necklace ■ 2012
29 x 19 x 15 cm
Sterling silver, fine silver, 18-karat
gold, 24-karat gold flakes, acrylic,
fiberglass, mixed media; handmade
PHOTOGRAPHY BY KAROLINA BIK

267

JOELLE SHAFTER
Felted Ruffle Necklace ■ 2011
25.4 x 25.4 x 1.2 cm
Vintage fur; hand felted, crocheted
PHOTOGRAPHY BY ALEXANDRA SHAFTER

SANDRA DONABED
Cigar Box Necklace ■ 2012

40 x 2 x 0.2 cm
Repurposed cigar boxes, found
wooden beads, waxed linen
PHOTOGRAPHY BY ARTIST

JACQUELINE RYAN
Neckpiece ■ 2010

50 x 3 x 3 cm
18-karat gold, vitreous enamel

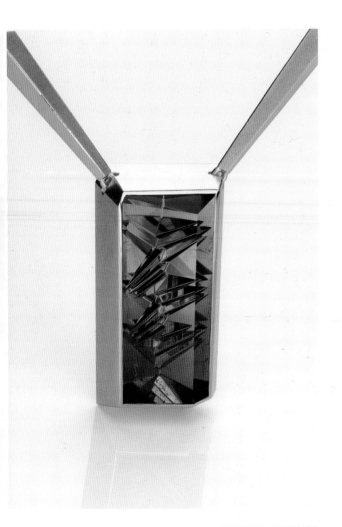

TOM MUNSTEINER
Bicolor Tourmaline Necklace ■ 2012
Pendant: 4 x 2 x 1.5 cm
Tourmaline, gold
PHOTOGRAPHY BY ARTIST

LINDA MACNEIL
Mesh Necklace ■ 2012
Pendant: 8.9 x 6.3 x 1.7 cm
Vitrolite glass, transparent glass, 24-karat
gold-plated mesh chain; acid polished
PHOTOGRAPHY BY BILL TRUSLOW

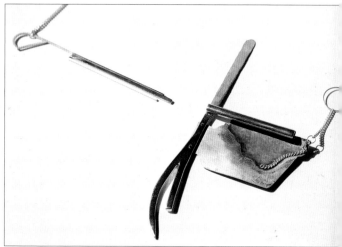

GAL KUPERMAN
Water Channel ■ 2011
Pendant: 12 x 9.3 x 0.7 cm
Sterling silver, enamel; fabricated
PHOTOGRAPHY BY RAN PLOTENIZKY AND SNIR KAZIR

ELLIOT GASKIN
Arrow of Pride ■ 2012
48.2 x 12.7 x 1.2 cm
Sterling silver, nickel silver,
brass, snakeskin, patina
PHOTOGRAPHY BY ARTIST

273

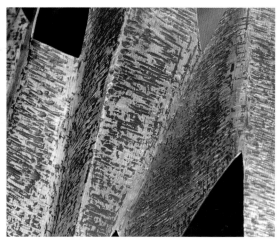

CHELSEA FAY
Fractal Collar ■ 2010
17.7 x 38.1 x 45.7 cm
Brass, acrylic; hand formed
and fabricated
PHOTOGRAPHY BY ELIZABETH TORGERSON-LAMARK

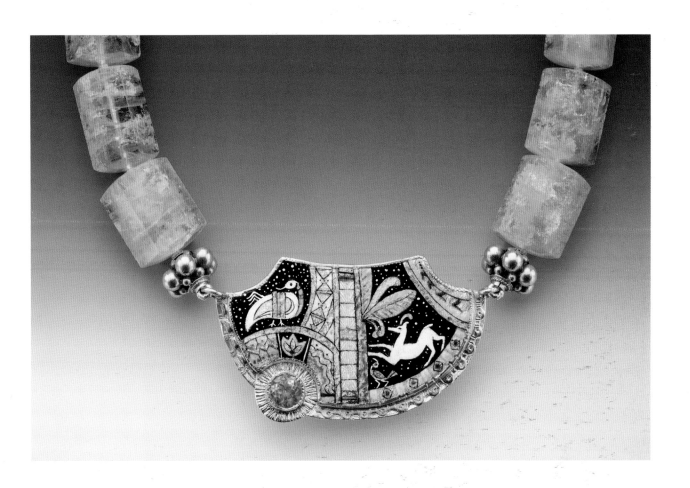

MARIANNE HUNTER
In the Golden Cradle ■ 2011
Centerpiece: 2.8 x 5 x 0.3 cm
24-karat gold, 22-karat gold, 14-karat gold, Argentium
silver, grisaille, enamel with 24-karat gold and pure silver
foil, sphalerite, beryls; polished, fabricated, engraved
PHOTOGRAPHY BY GEORGE POST

SAM GASSMAN
Cameo Necklace ■ 2012
25 x 10 x 1.5 cm
Found cameos, sterling silver,
vermeil; cast, fabricated
PHOTOGRAPHY BY ARTIST

LAURIE LEONARD
Acorn and Leaf Woman ■ 2010
50 x 40 x 5 cm
Pewter setting and clasp designed by
artist, reproduction of artist's drawing,
resin, silk cord; hand dyed, crimped
PHOTOGRAPHY BY LARRY SANDERS

277

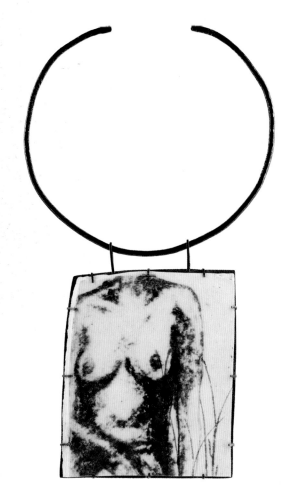

CHRISTINE SIMPSON-FORNI
Nude with Two Dancers ■ 2012
43 x 25 x 1 cm
Sterling silver, porcelain, mason
stains; planished, prong set, oxidized
PHOTOGRAPHY BY JAMES FORNI

SUE DAVIS
Ginkgo Meditation ■ 2012
Pendant: 7.6 x 3.8 x 1.9 cm
Stoneware clay, beach stone, photo image,
bamboo tile; hand formed, drilled, collaged
PHOTOGRAPHY BY STEVE VACHON

DEBORA K. JACKSON
Totally Hip! ■ 2012
18 x 1.2 x 0.5 cm
Hippopotamus teeth, polymer clay, African brass,
batik bone beads, snake vertebrae disks
PHOTOGRAPHY BY ARTIST

JOANNA HILL
Reflected Past Scaffolding Neckpiece ■ 2011
42 x 15 x 6 cm
Acrylic sheet, brass, steel cord, silver;
oxidized, laser etched, dyed, soldered,
powder coated, saw pierced, riveted
PHOTOGRAPHY BY TRISHA WARD

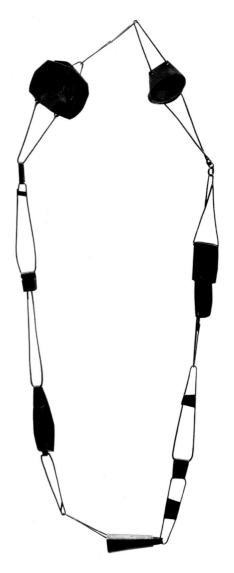

JOO YEON KIM
Mystery II ■ 2012
45 x 20 x 6 cm
Brass, plastic
PHOTOGRAPHY BY MYOUNG-WOOK HUH

GIOVANNI SICURO
Black ■ 2011
115 x 20 x 2 cm
Silver, niello; hollow constructed
PHOTOGRAPHY BY LAURA TESSARO

XIANOU NI
Moonlight Pendant ■ 2012
5.1 x 4.3 x 1.2 cm
Silver, 18-karat gold, pearl, citrine;
folded, soldered, fabricated, set
PHOTOGRAPHY BY ARTIST

FACING PAGE
BEVERLY TADEU
seed. pod ■ 2011
19 x 17.7 x 2.5 cm
Sterling silver, 18-karat
gold, 18-karat gold bimetal;
oxidized, forged, formed
PHOTOGRAPHY BY HAP SAKWA

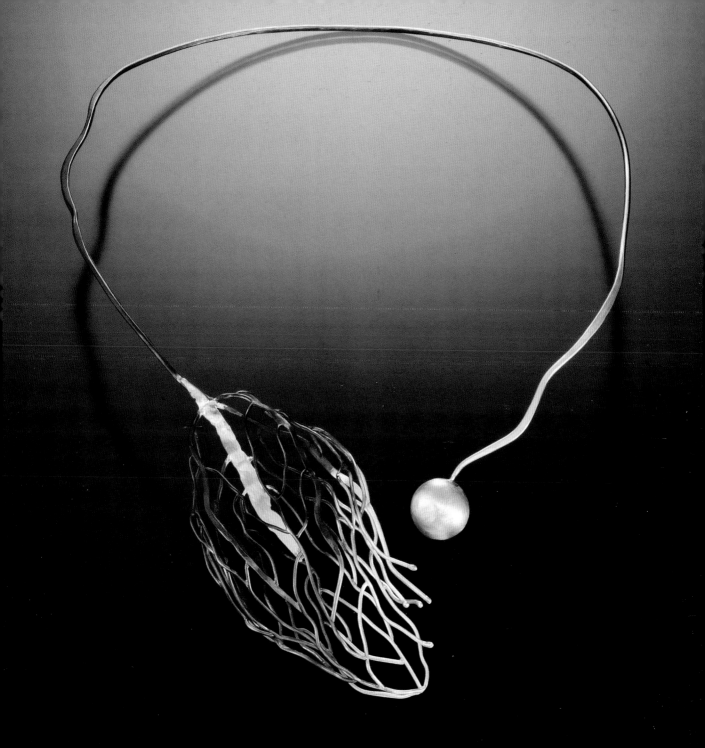

HYUNHEE LEE
Shark Is Not Scared ■ 2012
35 x 29 x 2 cm
Linden wood, marble, agate;
ironed, cold connected
PHOTOGRAPHY BY KOOKMIN UNIVERSITY STUDIO

KAREN VANMOL
Fading Landscape ■ 2011
45 x 8 x 3 cm
Wood, zinc, paint, cotton, glass,
acrylate, brass; mixed techniques
PHOTOGRAPHY BY ARTIST

BETH BLANKENSHIP
Domestic Goddess ■ 2007
12 x 12 x 12 cm
Clothespins, glass beads,
cord from a clothesline
PHOTOGRAPHY BY JESSICA STEPHENS

285

LOUISE RAUH
3 Flower Neckpiece ■ 2011
20.3 x 17.7 x 0.5 cm
Aluminum, freshwater pearls, peridot,
amethyst, ruby beads; hand painted
COLLABORATION WITH BETHANY YOUNG
PHOTOGRAPHY BY ARTIST

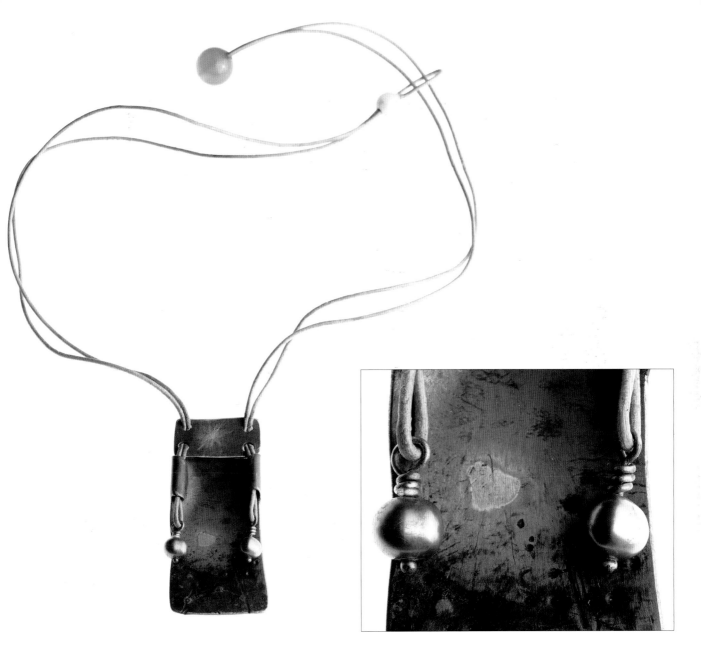

MARY ZAYMAN
Little World ■ 2012

Pendant: 7 x 2.5 cm
Copper, brass, leather cord, semiprecious
stone beads, cement, patina; fabricated,
oxidized, punched, hammered, textured
PHOTOGRAPHY BY ALEXANDER CROWE

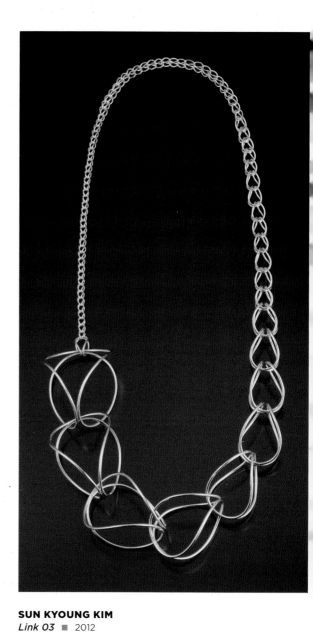

FRANCESCA URCIUOLI
Hands and Feet... ■ 2012
50 x 4 x 0.3 cm
Silver, ebony
PHOTOGRAPHY BY FEDERICO CAVICCHIOLI

SUN KYOUNG KIM
Link 03 ■ 2012
68 x 3.7 x 3.7 cm
Sterling silver, fine
silver, 18-karat gold
PHOTOGRAPHY BY ARTIST

JULIA LOWTHER
Byzantine Lace Collar ■ 2011

42 x 2.2 x 0.6 cm
Sterling silver; cast, custom
cut, hand linked
PHOTOGRAPHY BY DANIEL VAN ROSSEN

LESLIE D. BOYD
Crossed Legs ■ 2012
43 x 19 x 4.5 cm
Leather, clay, pantyhose,
cotton, filling, thread, steel
PHOTOGRAPHY BY ARTIST

ANNE E. MORGAN
Cotton Knot Necklace ■ 2012

45 x 3 x 2 cm
Brass, cotton
PHOTOGRAPHY BY SARAH J. THOMAS

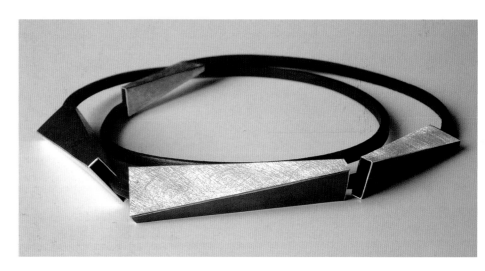

MELISSA FINELLI
Feeler Pendant ■ 2011
3 x 5.1 x 1.7 cm
Silver, 18-karat gold;
hand fabricated
PHOTOGRAPHY BY PETER HARRIS

CATERINA C. ZANCA
Surfaces ■ 2012
23 x 2 x 2 cm
Sterling silver, leather; oxidized,
soldered, hand fabricated
PHOTOGRAPHY BY ARTIST

SALLY PRANGLEY
Hammered Lace Necklace ■ 2012
53.3 x 3.8 cm
Annealed steel wire; hammered,
work hardened, linked
PHOTOGRAPHY BY ARTIST

293

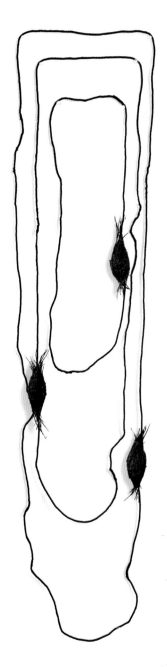

MARGARITA H. SAMPSON
Nestle ▪ 2012
140 x 25 x 10 cm
Found elastic, sterling-silver wire, found
twigs; stitched, hand woven
PHOTOGRAPHY BY CRAIG BENDER

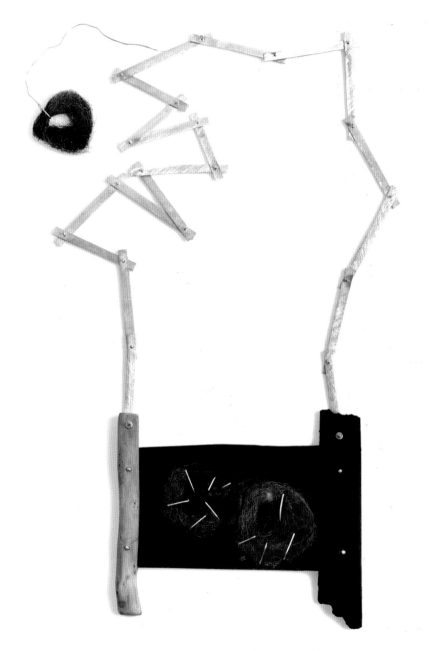

ALEJANDRA AGUSTI
Identity ■ 2011
40 x 11.5 x 1 cm
Silver, wood, nickel silver,
cattle hair; constructed
PHOTOGRAPHY BY PABLO MEHANNA

295

GABRI SCHUMACHER
Under My Skin ■ 2011
20 x 25 x 20 cm
Silicone, gold, diamonds
PHOTOGRAPHY BY ROB GLASTRA

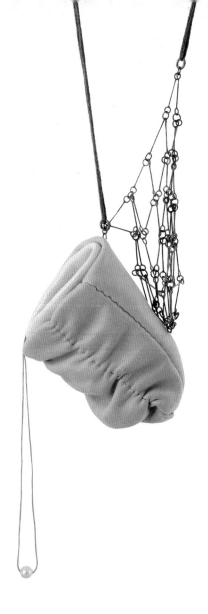

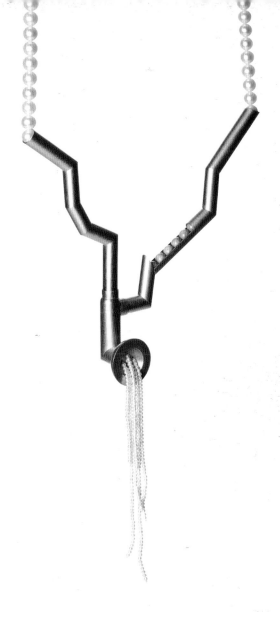

SOOYEON KIM
A Little Surprise ■ 2011
5 x 8 x 4 cm
Leather, sterling silver, 14-karat gold wire,
freshwater pearls, thread, yarn; hand cut, hand
stitched, soldered, punched, linked, pierced
PHOTOGRAPHY BY ARTIST

ANNETTE DAM
Filtered ■ 2010
Pendant: 16 x 15 x 3 cm
14-karat gold, gold-plated
silver, pearls, pink coral
PHOTOGRAPHY BY DORTE KROGH

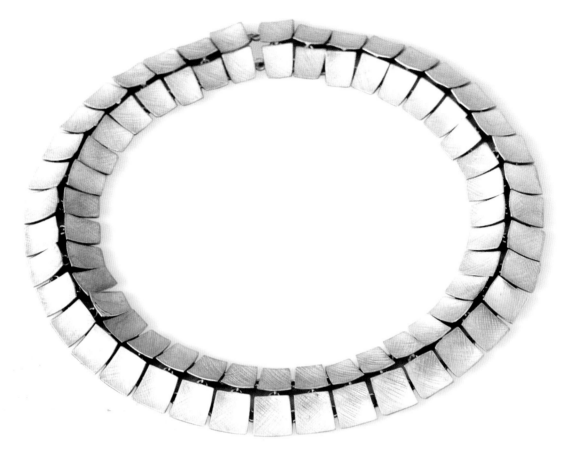

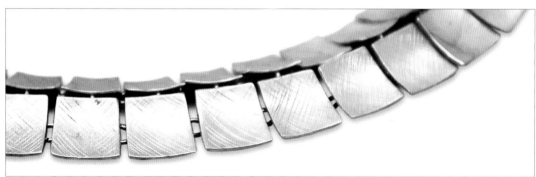

NELSON GABRIEL RIBEIRO
Town ■ 2010
45 x 23 cm
Silver, gold; handmade
PHOTOGRAPHY BY CÉSAR ISRAEL PAULO

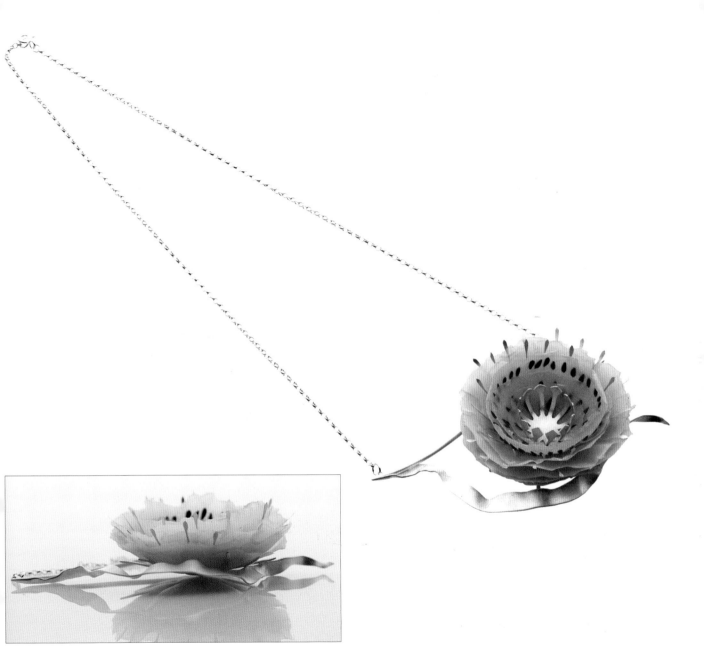

SABRINA MEYNS
Untitled ■ 2012
25 x 9 x 2.5 cm
Handmade paper, seeds,
silver; fabricated, riveted
PHOTOGRAPHY BY SYLVAIN DELEU

299

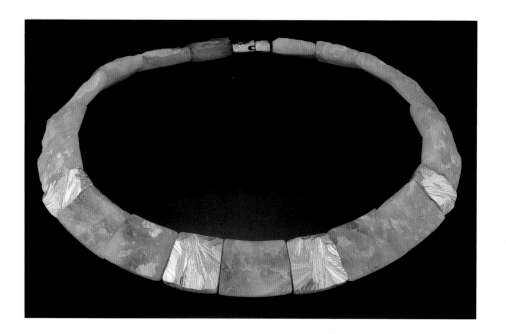

KLAUS SPIES
Aquamarine Necklace ■ 2012
45 x 3.5 x 2 cm
18-karat gold; hand
fabricated, cast
PHOTOGRAPHY BY LARRY SANDERS

CAROLYN A. YOUNG
Waves Necklace ■ 2011
15.5 x 14.5 x 1 cm
Sterling silver, marbled paper, acrylic,
nylon-coated sterling-silver cable; hand
fabricated, soldered, hammered, formed
PHOTOGRAPHY BY ARTIST

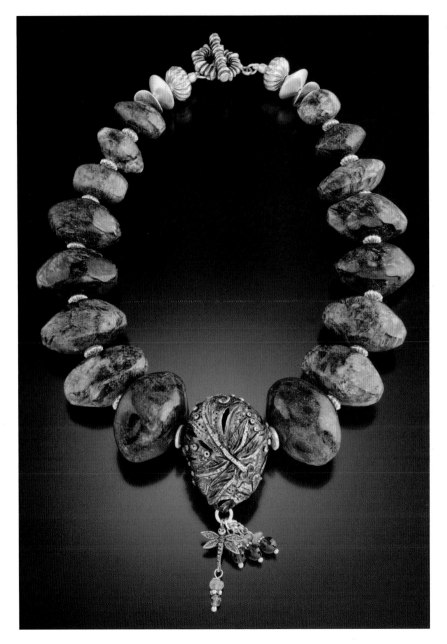

CANDICE WAKUMOTO
Linda's Dragonfly Charoite ■ 2010
45.7 x 5.6 x 2 cm
Silver clay, 22-karat gold, synthetic rubies, enamel paint, charoite,
amethyst, apatite, bronze, vermeil, sterling silver; hand formed
PHOTOGRAPHY BY LARRY SANDERS

JEN TOWNSEND
The Queen of the Night ■ 2010

34.2 x 16.5 x 3.3 cm
Sterling silver, diamonds, 14-karat palladium
white gold, patina; set, cast, fabricated
PHOTOGRAPHY BY HANK HENRY

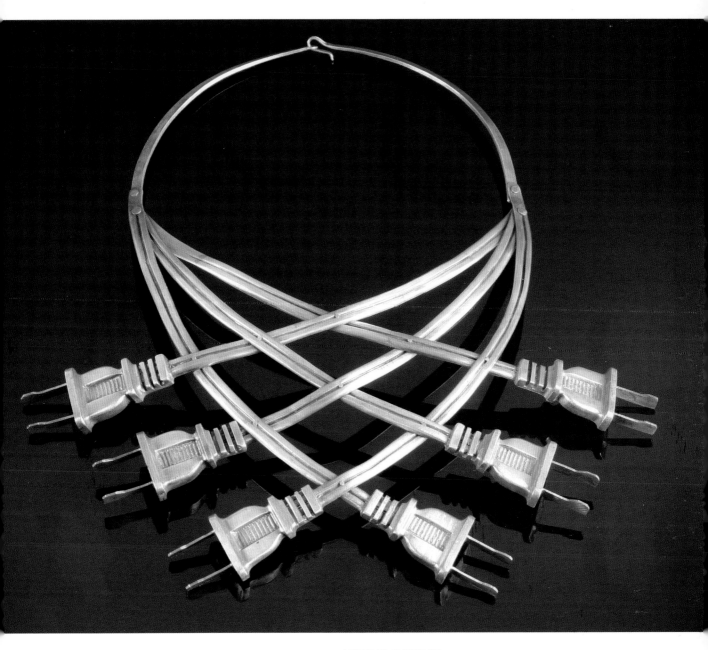

AIMEE M. HOWARD
Untitled ■ 2010
22.8 x 17.7 x 1.7 cm
Sterling silver; cast, fabricated
PHOTOGRAPHY BY ARTIST

LAURAN SUNDIN
Two Become One ■ 2010

60 x 20 x 4 cm
18-karat yellow gold, sterling silver, stainless
steel, saltwater pearls; oxidized, bobbin
lace techniques, hand woven, coiled
PHOTOGRAPHY BY ROBERT DIAMANTE

CAROL SALISBURY
Iron Necklace #2 ■ 2011
30.5 x 30.5 x 8.9 cm
Iron binding wire, brass, brazing
rod; woven, fabricated
PHOTOGRAPHY BY ARTIST

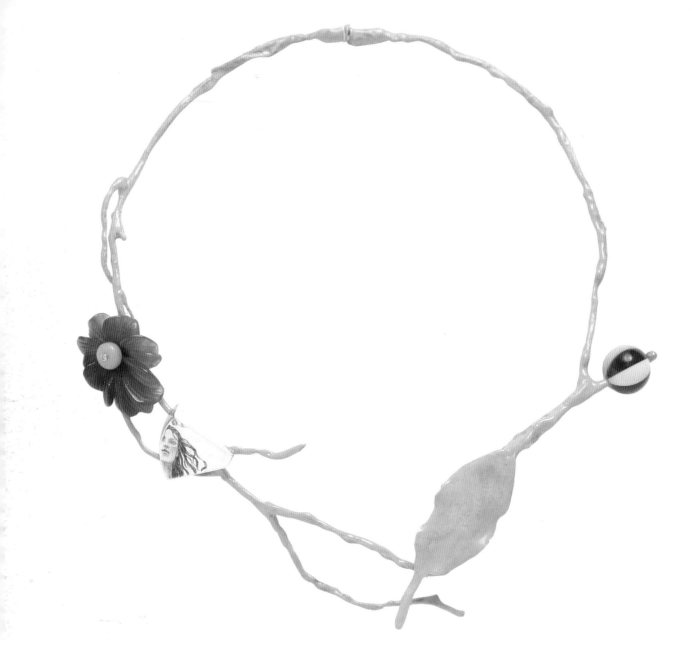

MADDALENA ROCCO
Collier Flora ■ 2010

25 x 20 x 5 cm
Enamel, carnelian, agate,
alexandrite, white gold;
ground, engraved
PHOTOGRAPHY BY ARTIST

KAMAL L. NASSIF
Ripe ■ 2012
27.9 x 5 x 0.3 cm
Acrylic, monofilament;
chemically fused, heat formed
PHOTOGRAPHY BY MARIAH TUTTLE

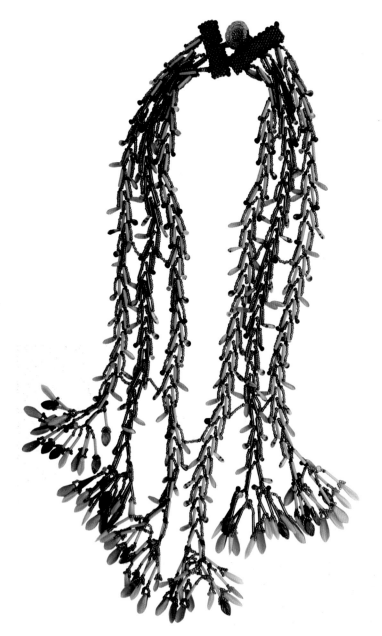

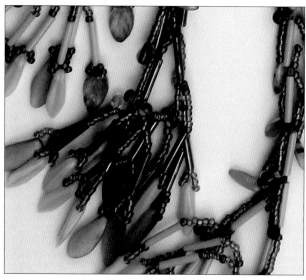

KOLBY FEHLBERG-BURNS
Waterfall Necklace ■ 2011

52 x 5.1 x 1 cm
Seed, bugle, dagger, and drop beads, vintage
button; modified herringbone stitch, peyote stitch
PHOTOGRAPHY BY ARTIST

DIANA FERGUSON
Opulent Triple Petal Pendant in Purple ■ 2012

Pendant: 7.6 x 7.6 x 1.7 cm
Watercolor paper, anodized aluminum, glass bead
accents, polyacrylic finish; hand cut, shaped, and woven
COLLECTION OF PAT KINDT
PHOTOGRAPHY BY ARTIST

ADRIENNE GASKELL
Green Kyanite Spike Necklace ■ 2007

50 x 8 cm
Green kyanite, carnelian, Swarovski crystals,
silver beads, glass beads, sterling-silver wire
PHOTOGRAPHY BY HAP SAKWA

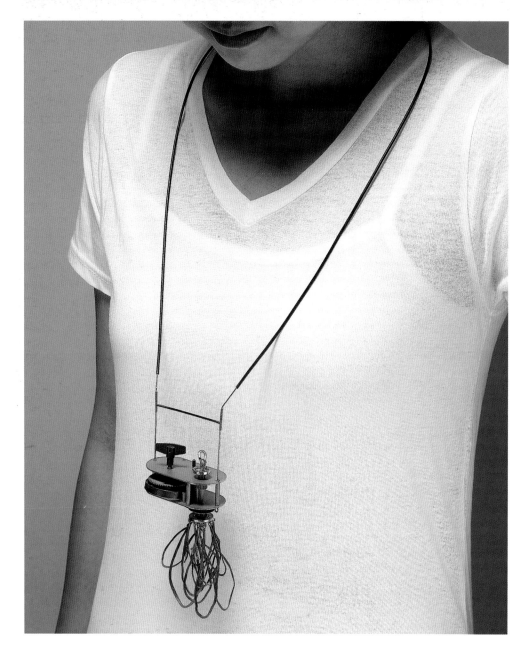

JUNSU KIM
Bloom ■ 2012
46 x 21 x 45 cm
Brass, nickel
PHOTOGRAPHY BY MUNCH STUDIO

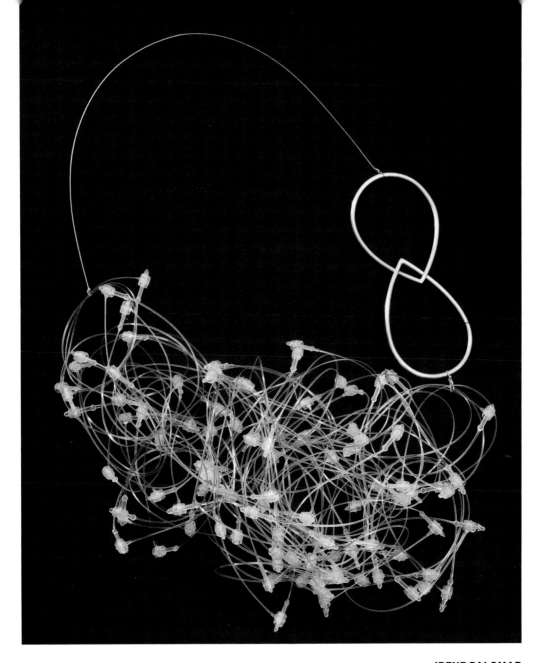

IRENE PALOMAR
Collar Gotas ■ 2011
25 x 18 cm
Silver, plastic; constructed
PHOTOGRAPHY BY DAMIÁN WASSER

LINDSAY FISHER
Wisdom ■ 2011
23 x 11 x 2 cm
Copper, bronze, plastic, glass, human
teeth, found objects; cast, fabricated,
electroformed, oxidized, pierced
PHOTOGRAPHY BY ARTIST

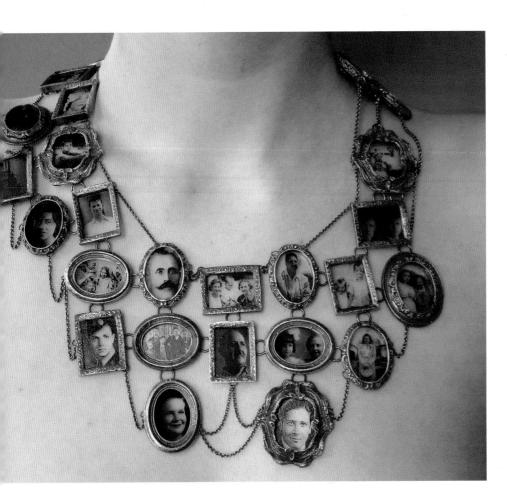

ASHLEY GILREATH
I Am Who They Were ■ 2011
26.6 x 20.3 cm
Sterling silver, bronze, glass
from microscope; cast
PHOTOGRAPHY BY MICHAEL WEBSTER

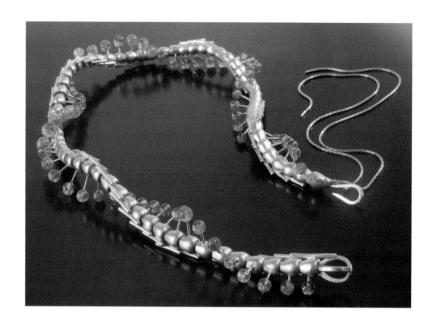

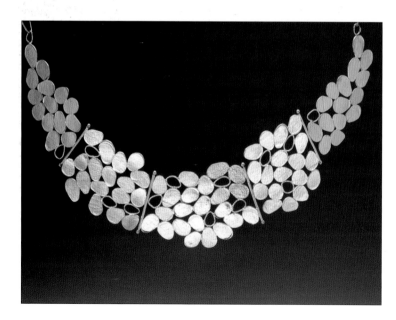

NANCY FINLEY
Pomegranate Love Necklace ■ 2012
57.2 x 3.8 x 0.1 cm
Sterling silver, 24-karat gold, fine
silver tubing and pins; rolled, textured,
soldered, assembled, keum boo
PHOTOGRAPHY BY CAROL HOLADAY

SHERIDAN KENNEDY
Helicula ■ 2010
38 x 2.5 x 2.5 cm
Sterling silver, labradorite;
CAD, cast, soldered
PHOTOGRAPHY BY SHINY OBJECTS PRODUCTIONS

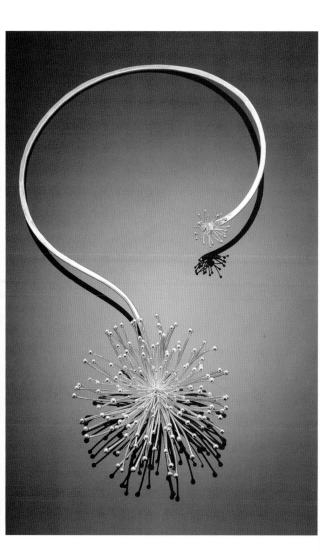

PAULETTE J. WERGER
Allium Neckpiece ■ 2011
40.6 x 35.5 x 7.6 cm
Sterling silver; fused, fabricated
PHOTOGRAPHY BY CHARLEY FREIBERG

315

JEFFREY L. DEVER
A Midsummer's Quest ■ 2011
13.9 x 11.4 x 1.7 cm
Polymer clay, nylon-coated
stainless steel, anodized niobium
PHOTOGRAPHY BY GREGORY R. STALEY

Showcase 500
art necklaces

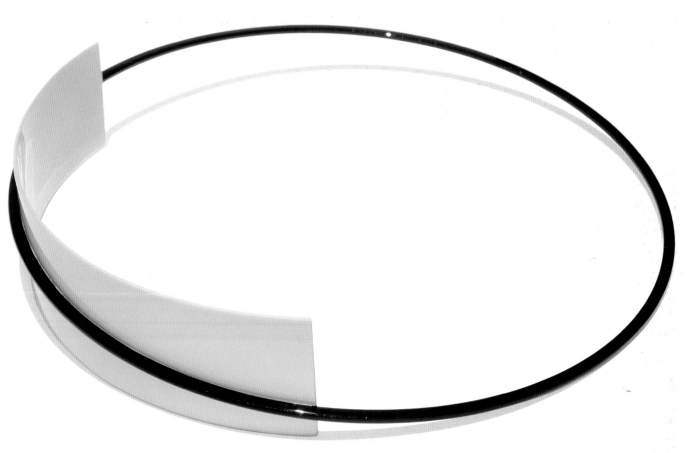

RACHELLE THIEWES
Slipstream ■ 2012
27.4 x 27.4 x 5 cm
Steel, automobile paint
PHOTOGRAPHY BY ARTIST

EVA SHERMAN
Sea Foam ■ 2012
25.4 x 20.3 x 2.5 cm
Sterling-silver wire, enameled
copper-wire tubular knit, sea glass
wire; wire worked, manipulated

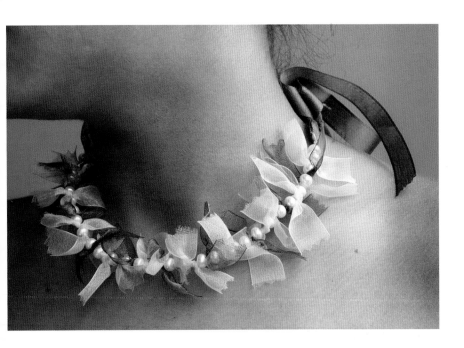

RANA DABIRI
Pearl ■ 2011
Overall length: 45 cm
Pearls, organza
PHOTOGRAPHY BY ARTIST

LUIS ACOSTA
Quipus ■ 2012
50 x 6 x 4 cm
Paper, thread; stitched
PHOTOGRAPHY BY ARTIST

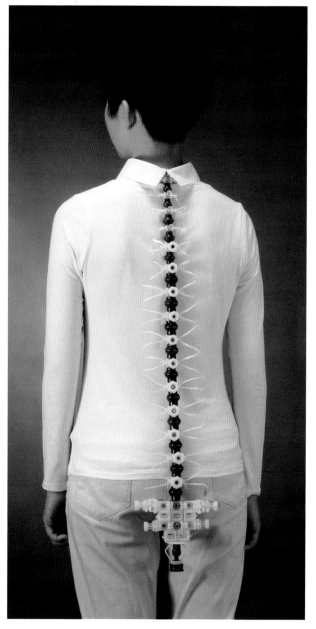

YU-LIN WANG
One-Seven Billionth–II ■ 2012

83 x 13 x 5 cm
Brass, cable clamps, cable tie, tie mounts, plastic
screws, dental floss, collar, button, sprinkler
PHOTOGRAPHY BY KUN-LONG CAI

DOLORES BARRETT
All Eyes Are upon You ■ 2012
4 x 4.5 x 1.5 cm
Fused glass, stainless steel wire,
sterling-silver chain; hand painted
PHOTOGRAPHY BY ARTIST

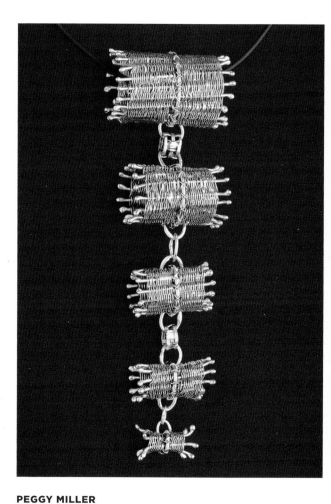

MARIA G. ERRAZURIZ
Trapelacuche Contemporaneo ■ 2012
Pendant: 15 x 10 x 5 cm
Silver, volcanic stone; embossed
PHOTOGRAPHY BY JEMK

PEGGY MILLER
Graduated Curler Necklace ■ 2012
Pendant: 6 x 3 x 1 cm
16-, 18-, and 22-gauge round silver wire,
28-gauge fine silver wire, patina; hand woven
PHOTOGRAPHY BY RYDER GLEDHILL

VALERIE A. OSTENAK
Vines and Tendrils ■ 2012
19 x 17.8 x 2.5 cm
Steel; forged, polished
PHOTOGRAPHY BY ARTIST

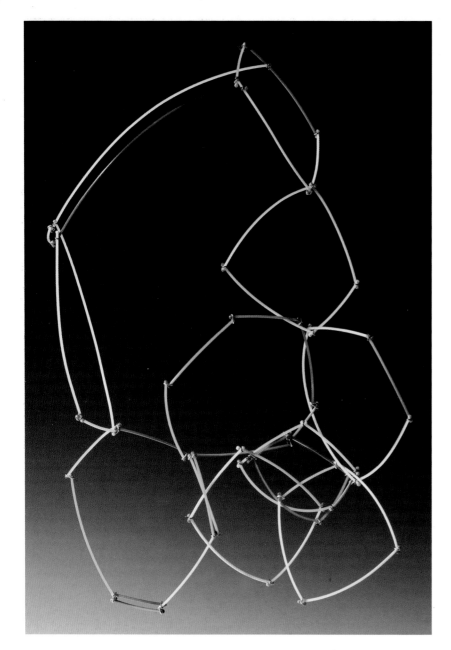

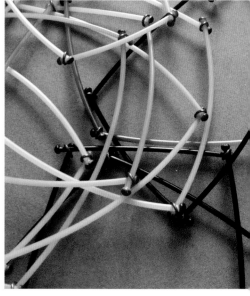

MARY DONALD
Backstory I ■ 2012
35.5 x 27.9 x 5 cm
Nylon, silver; oxidized,
dyed, formed, riveted
PHOTOGRAPHY BY ARTIST

JERA LODGE
Wicked ■ 2012

35.5 x 35.5 x 10.1 cm
Steel, merino wool, freshwater
pearls, cubic zirconia; needle felted
PHOTOGRAPHY BY HANNAH BAILEY

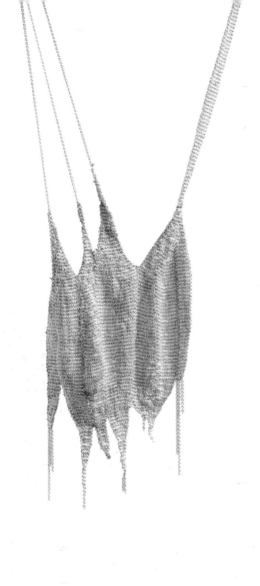

RIA E. LINS
Together ■ 2012
100 x 8 x 10 cm
Silver, thread; woven
PHOTOGRAPHY BY DRIES VAN DEN BRANDE

MAJA HOUTMAN
Sirkelidosia ■ 2012
50 x 5 x 5 cm
Silver, tourmaline
PHOTOGRAPHY BY A10DESIGN

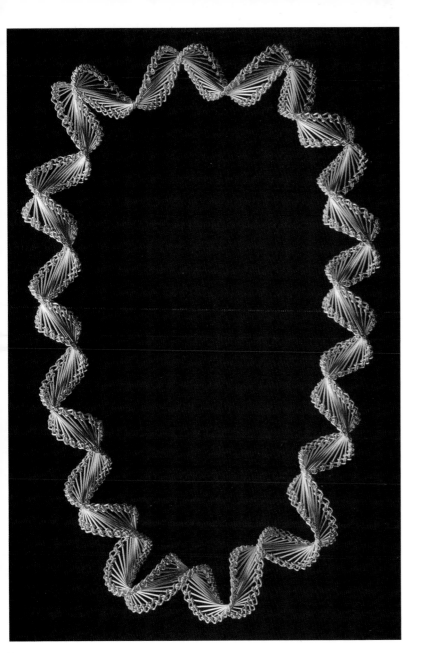

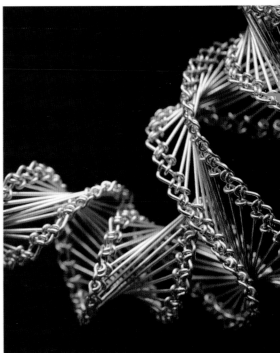

THORKILD H. THØGERSEN
Necklace ■ 2012
33 x 21.5 x 3 cm
Silver, wire; cut, bent
PHOTOGRAPHY BY ALEX BOZAS

ALEKSANDRA VALI
Revel of Bile and Envy ■ 2012
30 x 30 x 12 cm
Copper, lace; carved, cast,
metalsmithing, riveted,
hand fabricated
PHOTOGRAPHY BY ARTIST

Showcase 500
art necklaces

IRIS MISHLY
Mosquito Jewelry ▪ 2009

25 x 3.5 x 0.2 cm
Polymer clay, recycled mosquito mesh,
jewelry findings
PHOTOGRAPHY BY ARTIST

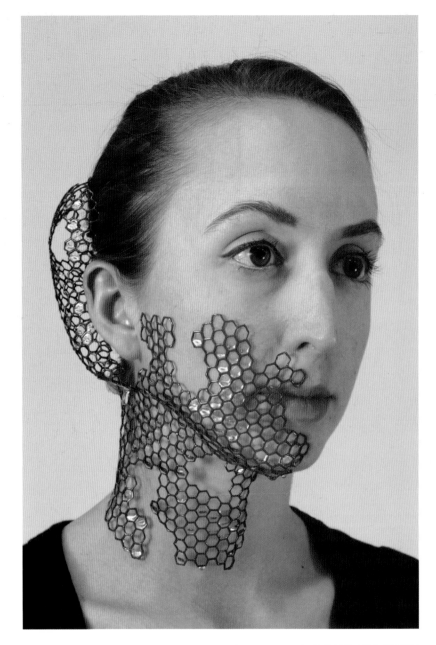

CHRISTIANA BYRNE
Hives ■ 2011
22.2 x 19.1 x 3.2 cm
Anodized aluminum and resin
PHOTOGRAPHY BY KEE-HO YUE

Showcase 500
art necklaces

LISA JOHNSON
Peanut Necklace, on the Go ■ 2011
40.6 x 29.2 x 3.8 cm
Slip-cast porcelain, sterling
silver, copper; fabricated
PHOTOGRAPHY BY ARTIST AND PHILLIP HARALAM

331

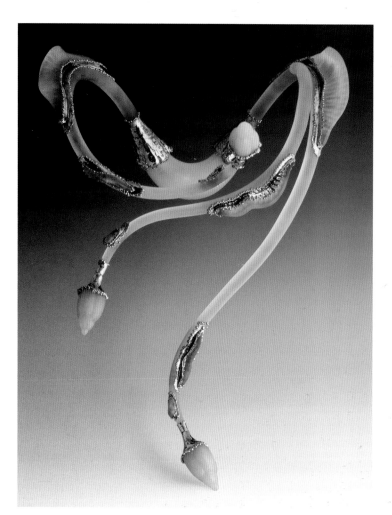
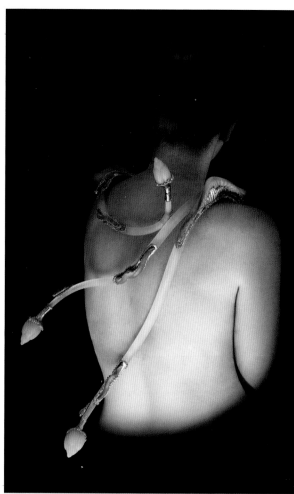

EMILY CULVER
Untitled ■ 2012
50.8 x 33 x 26.6 cm
Acrylic, copper, resin, silicone; heat
formed, electroformed, carved, cast
PHOTOGRAPHY BY ARTIST

Showcase 500
art necklaces

BARBARA A. UMBEL
Jellyfish Necklace ■ 2012
Centerpiece: 7.6 x 7.6 x 1.2 cm
14-karat yellow gold, sterling silver, turban shell
from the Indian Ocean, moonstone, crystal
quartz, freshwater pearls; forged, fabricated

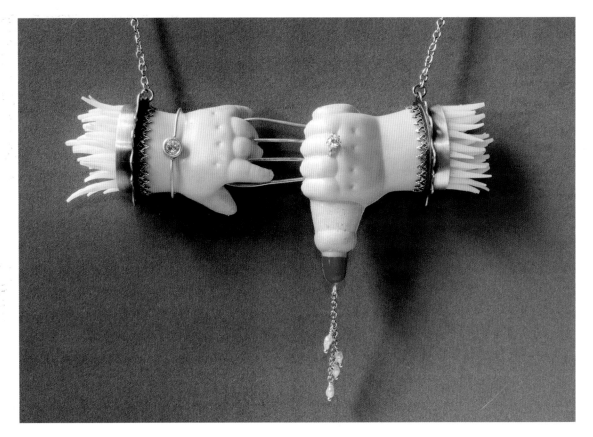

TESSA E. RICKARD
Mother's Milk ■ 2012
Pendant: 11 x 16 x 4 cm
Sterling silver, plastic, tusk shells,
cubic zirconia, nickel, stainless steel;
constructed, soldered, oxidized
PHOTOGRAPHY BY TIM CARPENTER

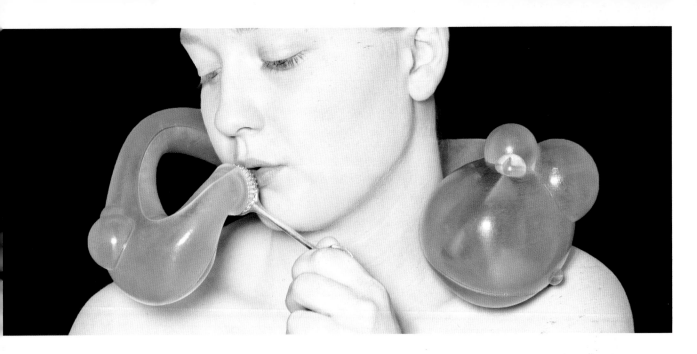

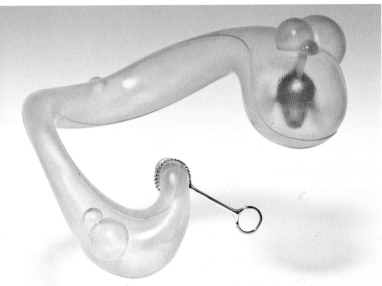

EMILY M. COBB
Billy's Bubble Blower ■ 2011
40.6 x 12.7 x 30.4 cm
Photopolymer, sterling silver
PHOTOGRAPHY BY ARTIST

SUSAN YACOUB
Isis, Queen of Goddesses ◼ 2012
42 x 19 x 2.5 cm
Swarovski crystal rivolis, bicones, pearls, Miyuki seed beads,
sheepskin and snakeskin leather base; bead embroidered,
peyote stitch, stop stitch, edge stitch, fringing, handmade
PHOTOGRAPHY BY ARTIST

BETSY BAKER
Red Daisy ■ 2012
Pendant: 5.1 x 5.1 cm
Polymer clay, vermeil, metallic paint, mica powders,
re-purposed earring; hollow construction
PHOTOGRAPHY BY ARTIST

STEVEN FORD
DAVID FORLANO
Tube Necklace #9 ■ 2010
18 x 2 x 2 cm
Polymer clay, sterling silver
PHOTOGRAPHY BY ARTISTS

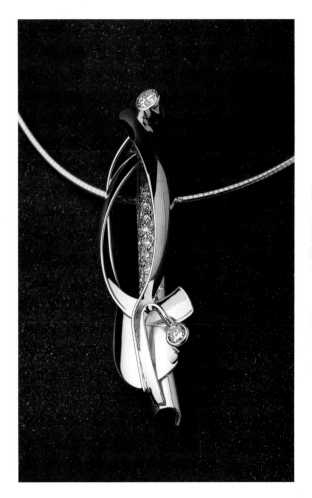

MICHAEL ALEXANDER
Mini Bibs 633 ■ 2012
Each pendant: 1.5 cm in diameter
18-karat yellow gold, 18-karat rose
gold, diamonds, sapphires; wax cast
PHOTOGRAPHY BY RALPH GABRINER

VEERLE VAN WILDER
Lily ■ 2011
75 x 25 x 2 cm
18-karat gold, diamonds; hand forged
PHOTOGRAPHY BY LUC VAN MUYLEM

FRANCISCA BAUZA
Abnäher Patrón II ■ 2010
45 x 24 x 8 cm
Copper, enamel, silver;
milled, hand sawed, cast
PHOTOGRAPHY BY ARTIST

EVELYN MARKASKY
Dangerous Vagina Necklace ■ 2011

50.8 x 1.8 cm
Copper, enamel; torch
fired, fold formed
PHOTOGRAPHY BY ARTIST

LARITZA D. GARCIA

Orange Crush Necklace ■ 2012

35.5 x 15.2 x 5 cm
Copper, steel, brass; powder
coated, hand pierced, formed,
fabricated, wire wrapped
PHOTOGRAPHY BY TARA LOCKLEAR

TIA KRAMER

Palpitation Series Necklace ■ 2011

53.3 x 11.9 x 4.3 cm
Sterling silver, handmade
paper; oxidized
PHOTOGRAPHY BY HANK DREW

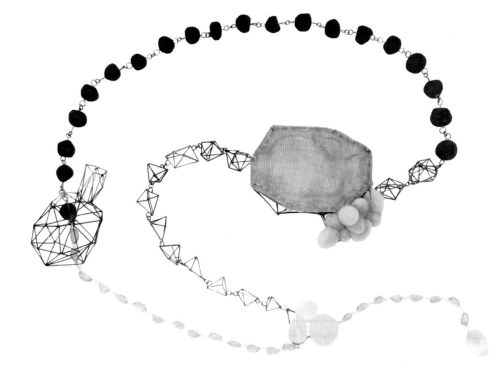

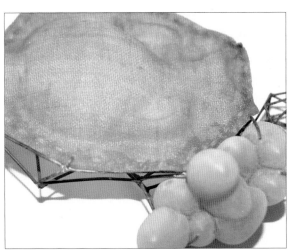

KATJA TOPORSKI
Eulogia 4 ■ 2012

60 x 12 x 3 cm
Silver, iron ore, silk, gelatin,
resin, linen, myrrh, wax
PHOTOGRAPHY BY ARTIST

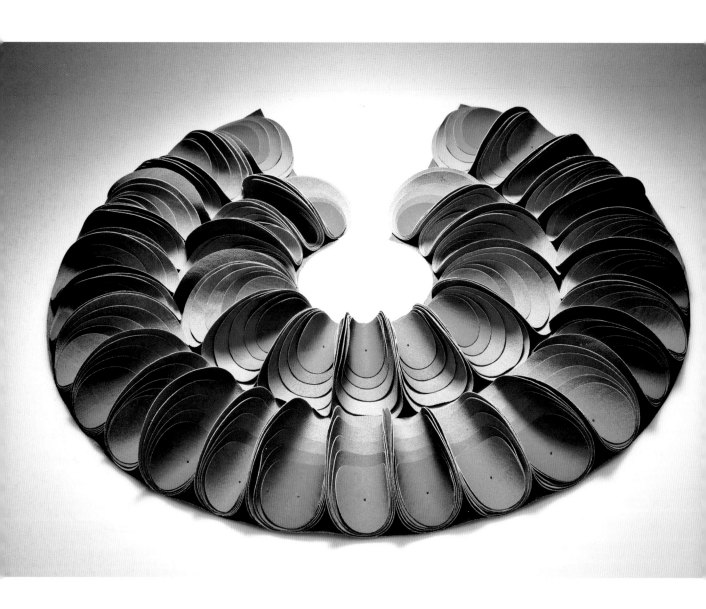

MARIAN ACOSTA CONTRERAS
Fusion Neckpiece ■ 2010
48 x 48 x 5 cm
Acrylic, canvas
PHOTOGRAPHY BY JINKYUN AHN

Showcase 500
art necklaces

EFHARIS ALEPEDIS
*Red Patent-Leather Necklace with
Silk Cocoons* ■ 2010

25.5 x 25.5 x 5 cm
Patent leather, silk cocoons, rubber,
sterling silver, epoxy resin, magnets
PHOTOGRAPHY BY MARK JOHNSTON

345

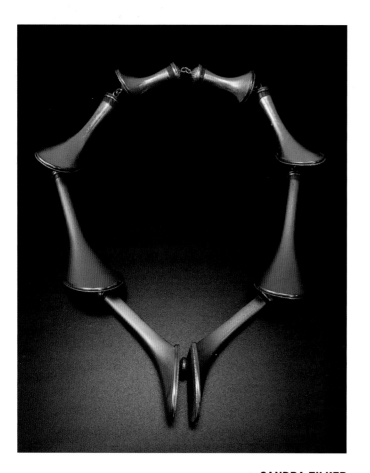

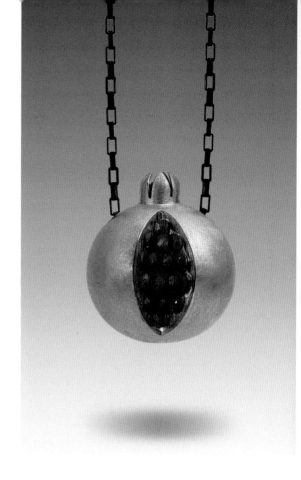

SANDRA ZILKER
Gold Heel Collar ■ 2012
35.5 x 20.3 x 5 cm
Recycled shoe heels, bronze;
etched, fabricated
PHOTOGRAPHY BY JACK ZILKER

BOLINE STRAND
Punica Granatum Necklace ■ 2011
Pendant: 2.8 x 2.2 x 2.2 cm
18-karat gold, faceted ruby
beads, sterling-silver chain,
18-karat gold clasp; beaded
PHOTOGRAPHY BY BARRY BLAU

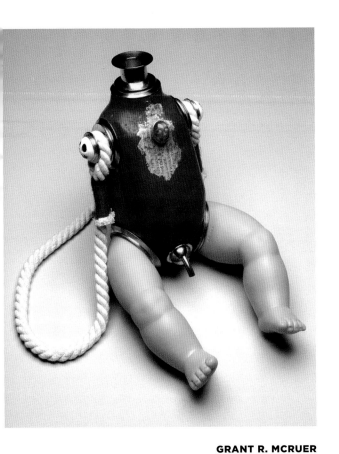

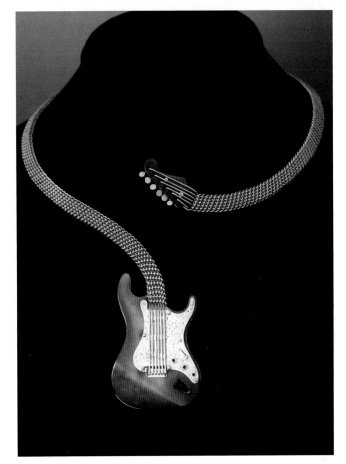

GRANT R. MCRUER
Post-Apocalyptic Peeing Doll ■ 2011
26 x 11 x 6 cm
Papier-mâché, doll parts, brass, enamel,
moonstone, silver, paint, rope
PHOTOGRAPHY BY ARTIST

JENNIFER HANSCOM
Guitar Necklace ■ 2010
Guitar body: 6 x 3.5 x 0.6 cm
Sterling silver, patina, copper; woven,
fabricated, riveted, lacquered, textured
PHOTOGRAPHY BY ARTIST

347

LESLIE SHERSHOW
Rain ■ 2012
30 x 12 x 1 cm
Sterling silver, acrylic, veneer, brass,
walnut, purpleheart, vintage fishing
line; fabricated, oxidized, polished
PHOTOGRAPHY BY ARTIST

KIMBERLY WINKLE
Red Pendant Horsehair
Necklace ■ 2012

Pendant: 6 x 3 x 3 cm
Polychrome mahogany, horsehair,
rubber; lathe turned
PHOTOGRAPHY BY JOHN LUCAS

349

JEONGHYE PARK
Voyaging Castle ■ 2012
55 x 12 x 5.5 cm
Sterling silver, silk, cubic
zirconia; fabricated, oxidized
PHOTOGRAPHY BY MYUNG-WOOK HUH

JUDITH E. RENSTROM
Box Chain ■ 2011
29 x 19 x 22 cm
23-karat gold, sterling silver;
keum boo, fabricated, oxidized
PHOTOGRAPHY BY HUB WILLSON

Showcase **500**
art necklaces

JANET CRAMPTON PIPES

Orbit II Necklace ■ 2012

50.8 x 1.3 x 0.5 cm
Sterling silver, 22-karat gold, 18-karat gold, sterling
silver and 22-karat gold bimetal, opal, patina;
hand knit, etched, roll printed, fabricated, riveted
PHOTOGRAPHY BY GEORGE POST

351

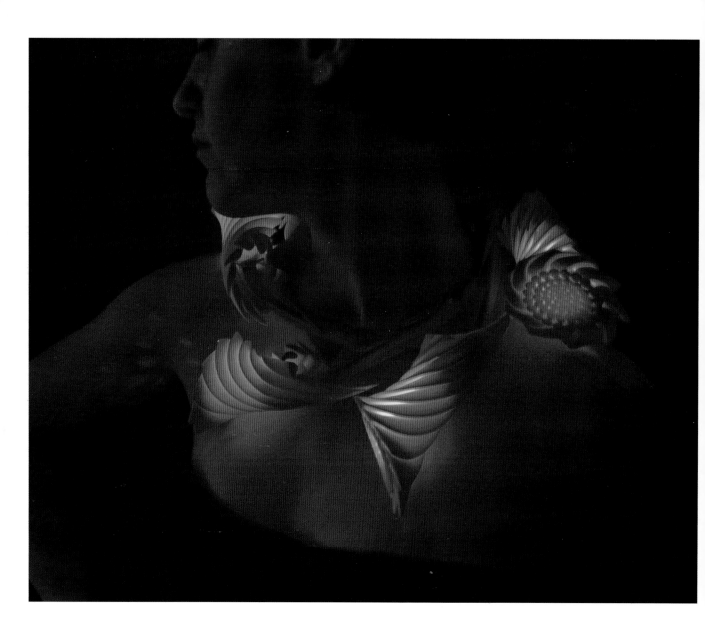

JOCELYN KOLB
Inflorillumini ■ 2010
35 x 35 x 10 cm
Resin, light-emitting diodes;
3D modeled and printed
PHOTOGRAPHY BY ARTIST

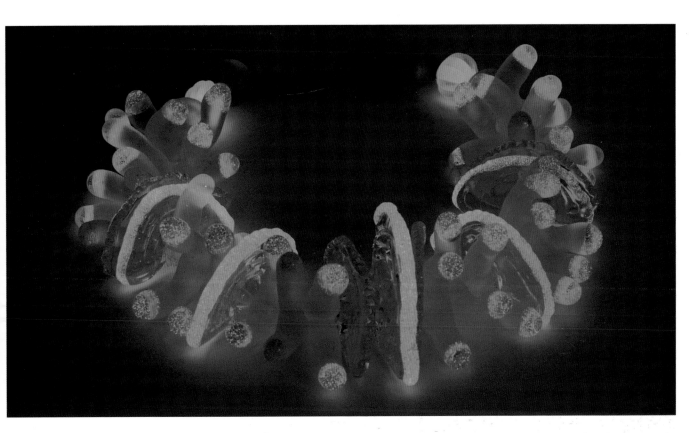

KATE ROTHRA FLEMING

Ocean Necklace ■ 2012

45.7 x 5.1 x 5.1 cm
Soda-lime glass, dichroic glass,
phosphorescent glass, sterling
silver; oxidized, torch formed
PHOTOGRAPHY BY RICK RHODES

FACING PAGE
IRIS LEE
Fantasy Corset Choker ■ 2011

9 x 30 x 5 cm
Wire, crystals, freshwater
pearls, beads; wire wrapped,
beaded, woven
PHOTOGRAPHY BY ARTIST

PATTY TIRY
Midas ■ 2011

40.6 x 15.2 x 2.5 cm
Swarovski crystals, pearls,
glass seed beads
PHOTOGRAPHY BY LARRY SANDERS

355

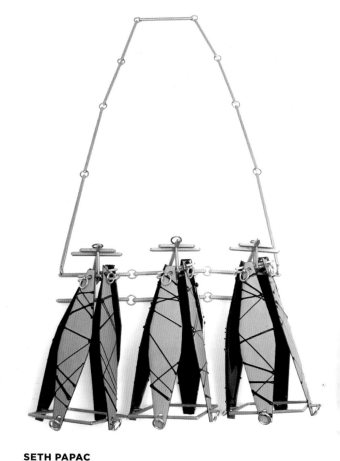

ALEXANDRA S. PEREZ DEMMA
Waste ■ 2011

71.1 x 30.4 x 6.3 cm
Copper, enamel, brass,
steel wire; fabricated
PHOTOGRAPHY BY SETH PAPAC

SETH PAPAC
Put on the Lights ■ 2011

35 x 17 x 7 cm
Copper, brass; enameled, fabricated
PHOTOGRAPHY BY ARTIST

UTE DECKER
Architect's Necklace ■ 2011
75 x 0.2 x 0.2 cm
Sterling silver, stainless
steel cable; fabricated
PHOTOGRAPHY BY ARTIST

357

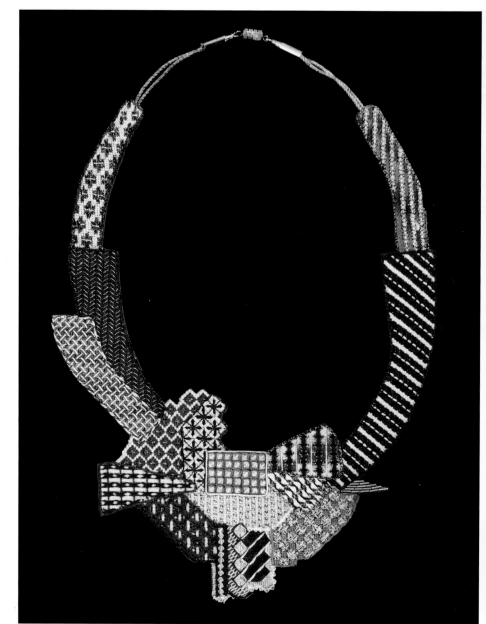

MARTY JONAS
Summertime ■ 2011
26.6 x 18.2 x 0.5 cm
Silk and metallic threads, beads,
crystals, suede-like material,
silver findings; needlepoint
PHOTOGRAPHY BY ARTIST

MARCELA PÈREZ
Corales ■ 2012
30 x 24 x 1 cm
Cotton, fiber; crochet
PHOTOGRAPHY BY JUAN CRUZ COROMINAS

SALLY CRAIG
Bead Necklace ■ 2010
Overall length: 40 cm
22-karat gold, 18-karat gold, sterling
silver, fine silver, lava beads; oxidized,
hand woven and fabricated
PHOTOGRAPHY BY RALPH GABRINER

Showcase 500
art necklaces

SO YOUNG PARK
Dreaming Tree ■ 2012
Pendant: 5 x 7 x 1 cm
Silver, tourmaline, garnet, peridot, citrine,
labradorite; chased, soldered, oxidized
PHOTOGRAPHY BY ARTIST

ANNALEENA SOINI
Ego Sum Qui Sum ■ 2011
Pendant: 3 x 3 x 0.7 cm
Sterling silver; goldsmithing
PHOTOGRAPHY BY SILTANEN KIMMO

BARBARA HEINRICH
Peruvian Opal and Diamond Necklace ■ 2011

45.7 x 4.4 x 0.6 cm
Peruvian opal slices, 18-karat yellow gold, diamonds; bezel set, hand fabricated
PHOTOGRAPHY BY HAP SAKWA

363

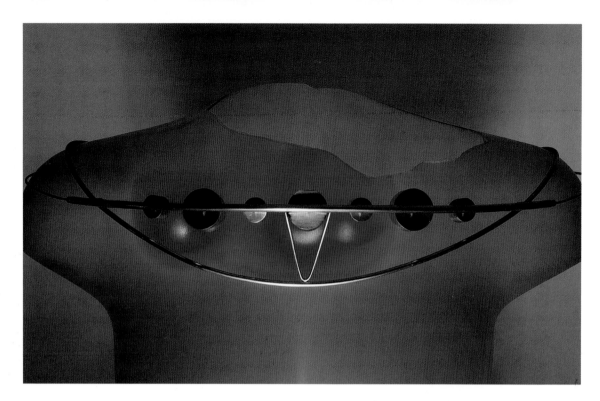

ERINA KASHIHARA
The Shadows in the Foreground ■ 2012
11.5 x 34 x 24 cm
Silver, brass, electric circuit,
battery, light-emitting diode
PHOTOGRAPHY BY KEIICHI TANAKA

KAREN MOON
Worms Necklace ■ 2012
9 x 10 x 2.5 cm
Epoxy resin, nylon
monofilament; cast
PHOTOGRAPHY BY ALLISTER MOON AND ARTIST

MISUN WON
*Jogakbo Wrapping
Pendant* ■ 2010

8 x 8 x 2 cm
Sterling silver, braided
silk cord; hand cut
PHOTOGRAPHY BY ARTIST

CAROLYN ZAKARIJA
Ladinelli Necklace ■ 2012

Pendant: 5.5 x 1.8 x 0.8 cm
Sterling silver, 14-karat gold, lava, coral,
pearl; folded, domed, hand stamped
PHOTOGRAPHY BY RALPH GABRINER

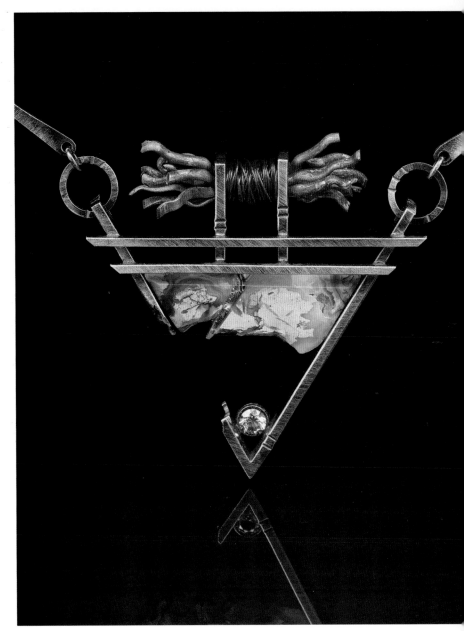
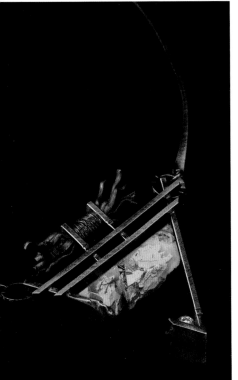

MARC ZOSCHKE
WENDY ZOSCHKE
Forever ■ 2011

Pendant: 6.3 x 6.3 x 1.3 cm
Fused glass, rough stone, copper, silver,
white sapphire; inlaid, cut, beveled, polished
PHOTOGRAPHY BY ARTISTS

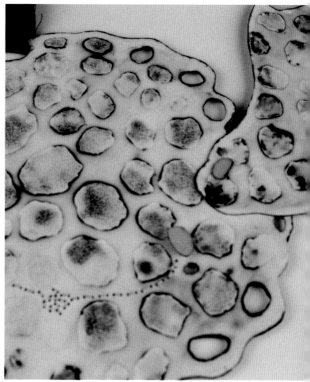

SATOMI KAWAI
Connection and Division VIII ■ 2011
55 x 20 x 1 cm
Steel, pigment, sterling silver,
cotton thread, organza; soldered,
etched, blackened, sewed
PHOTOGRAPHY BY ARTIST

DEBRA DOWDEN-CROCKETT
Ode to the Doodle ■ 2011

45.7 x 12.7 x 7.6 cm
Glass, steel, copper; torch worked,
hand sculpted and shaped
PHOTOGRAPHY BY ARTIST

WENDOLYN HAMMER WHITE
Sea Bubbles ■ 2011
45 x 6.2 x 1.2 cm
Found rock, silver, turquoise, white topaz,
peridot; inlaid, tension mounted, bezel set
PHOTOGRAPHY BY DEAN POWELL

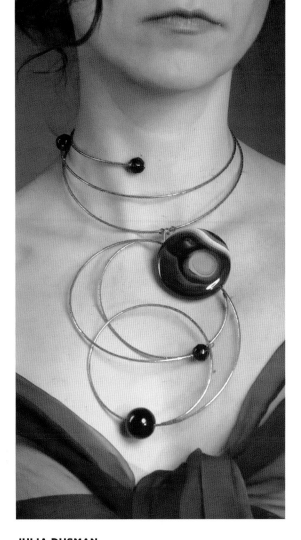

ÅSA LOCKNER
Crown Jewels No. 8 ■ 2012
23 x 15 x 1 cm
Silver, smoky quartz, enamel;
sawed, constructed
PHOTOGRAPHY BY MATS HÅKANSON

JULIA DUSMAN
Zodiac ■ 2011
25 x 12 x 1.5 cm
Purple agate, fluorite,
Swarovski crystal, glass, wire
PHOTOGRAPHY BY JENS LOOK

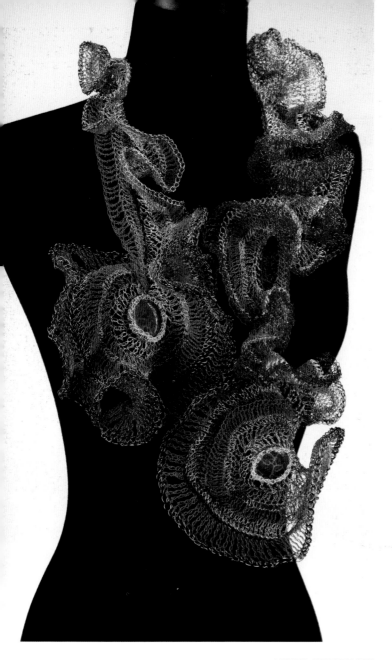

AMBER O'HARROW
Abuse of a Rainbow through Crochet ▪ 2009

66 x 28 x 10 cm
Anodized aluminum and copper wire,
fire agate beads; crocheted

PHOTOGRAPHY BY ARTIST

Showcase 500
art necklaces

LISA KLAKULAK
Sheath ■ 2011
25.4 x 27.9 x 2.5 cm
Merino wool fleece, silk and tulle fabric,
cotton sewing thread; needle and wet felted,
fused, free-motion machine embroidered
PHOTOGRAPHY BY MARY VOGEL

373

MIKEL ROBINSON
Dominae ■ 2011
Pendant: 7.6 x 5.7 x 3.1 cm
Wooden box, mica sheet, brass nails, Victorian clock keys, etched brass, dirt, annealed steel, leather, eighteenth-century missal paper, nineteenth-century marbled paper, paper, linen thread; hand formed

DANA B. STENSON
*Georgia Helen Griffith: A Portrait of the
Artist's Great-Grandmother* ▨ 2011

Locket: 10.3 x 5.1 cm
Copper, sterling silver, garnet, sapphires, found
objects, resin; etched, cast, formed, fabricated
PHOTOGRAPHY BY JOHN DOWLING

375

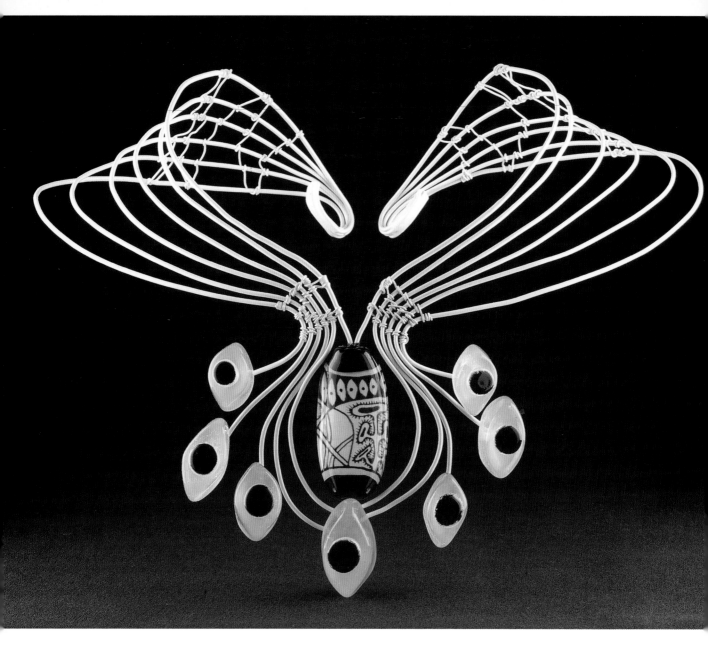

BRONWEN HEILMAN
In Transit ■ 2012

40.6 x 33 cm
Recycled glass, Italian glass, vitreous
enamels, steel; powder coated,
flameworked, hand fabricated
PHOTOGRAPHY BY DOUG BALDWIN

RALPH BAKKER
Sensual ■ 2011
25 x 15 x 4 cm
Gold, silver, enamel, pearls
PHOTOGRAPHY BY MICHAEL ANHALT

NANZ AALUND
Crystal Cross ■ 2011
Pendant: 5 x 5 x 2 cm
Sterling silver, amethyst
PHOTOGRAPHY BY DOUG YAPLE

MARIEL PAGLIAI
Unstructured ■ 2012
5.2 x 4.8 x 0.8 cm
Sterling silver, pearls, topaz
PHOTOGRAPHY BY ARTIST

TOM MUNSTEINER
Aquamarine Necklace ■ 2012
Pendant: 4.5 x 2.5 x 1.5 cm
Aquamarine, spirit diamond, platinum
PHOTOGRAPHY BY ARTIST

JUDITH S. PYLE
Queen of Hearts ■ 2001
Overall length: 58.4 cm
Sterling silver, found tins,
copper, ruby, patina; fabricated,
hydraulic pressed
PHOTOGRAPHY BY JOSEPH HYDE

Showcase 500
art necklaces

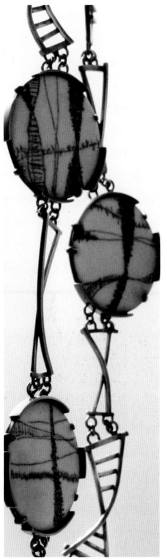

L. SUE SZABO
Destination ■ 2011
30.5 x 12.7 x 0.8 cm
Sterling silver, enamel on copper,
graphite; hand fabricated, prong
set, kiln fired, drawn, stoned
PHOTOGRAPHY BY ERICKA CRISSMAN

SIBYLLE FLOURET
Untitled ■ 2011
20 x 26 x 2.5 cm
Tampons, cotton, brass
PHOTOGRAPHY BY ARTIST

Showcase 500
art necklaces

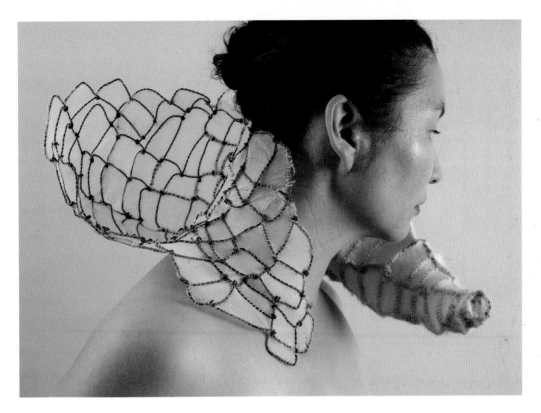

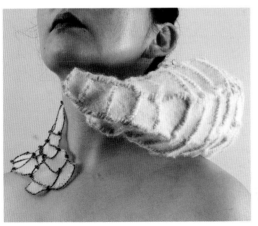
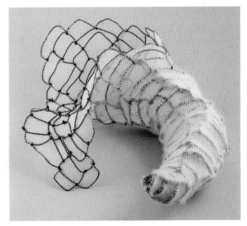

LYDIA T. HALL
Reverberation Horn ■ 2012
17.7 x 50.8 x 35.5 cm
Steel wire, wool, silk, thread; felted
PHOTOGRAPHY BY ARTIST

383

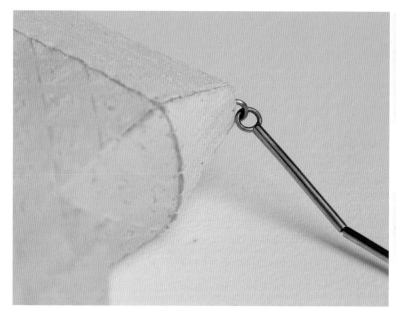

KARIN MAISCH
Hero ■ 2012
50 x 10 x 3 cm
Brass, textile; paint techniques,
sewed, cut, soldered
PHOTOGRAPHY BY ARTIST

SIMONA MOTUZAITE-KANDRATAVICIENE
Drink Me, Alice! ■ 2012
30 x 14 x 2.5 cm
Teabags, dried echinacea purpurea,
sterling-silver chain
PHOTOGRAPHY BY ARTIST

385

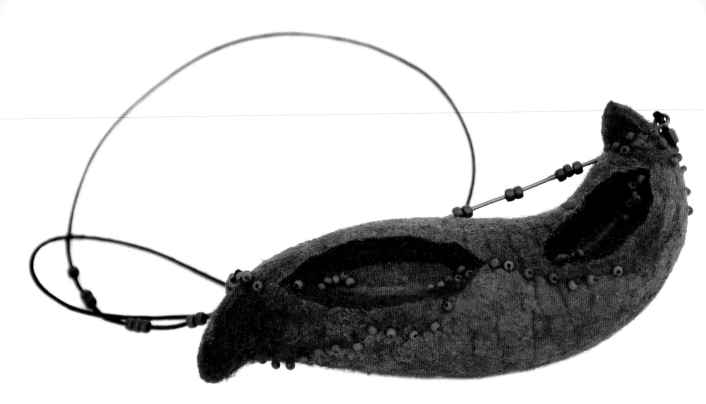

MARTIEN VAN ZUILEN
Cocoon ■ 2011
Pendant: 6 x 11 x 3 cm
Merino wool, silks, copper wire,
beads; hand felted, carved
PHOTOGRAPHY BY ARTIST

JENNIFER FECKER
Ribbon Neckpiece ■ 2011
21.6 x 21.6 x 1.3 cm
Wool felt; hand cut and assembled
PHOTOGRAPHY BY LAURA NASH

LINDA VAN ALSTYNE
Hidden Connections ■ 2012
Pendant: 4 x 1 x 4 cm
Merino wool, silk cord, magnetic
clasp; hand dyed, sculpted
PHOTOGRAPHY BY ARTIST

STEFANIE SHEEHAN
Peeking Eyes Neckpiece ■ 2012
27 x 22 x 2 cm
Brass, copper, flocking, taxidermy
eyes; formed, planished, chased
PHOTOGRAPHY BY DAVID BUTLER

LAUREN SIMEONI
Gingering Neckpiece ■ 2011

30 x 20 x 5 cm
Artificial plant foliage,
sterling silver, coral, shell,
glass beads; constructed
PHOTOGRAPHY BY RACHEL HARRIS

389

GLORIA DANVERS
A Flutter of Butterflies ■ 2012
Overall length: 55.9 cm
Polymer clay; twisted, pierced
PHOTOGRAPHY BY LARRY BERMAN

MARION DELARUE
Imprints ■ 2010
22 x 21 x 3.5 cm
Porcelain, wool;
hand pressed
PHOTOGRAPHY BY ARTIST

MARY ANN HELMOND
Flight of the Peacock ■ 2012
42 x 3 x 1 cm
Beads, antique copper findings, Swarovski
crystals, wire; lampworked, strung
PHOTOGRAPHY BY THOMAS WRIGHT

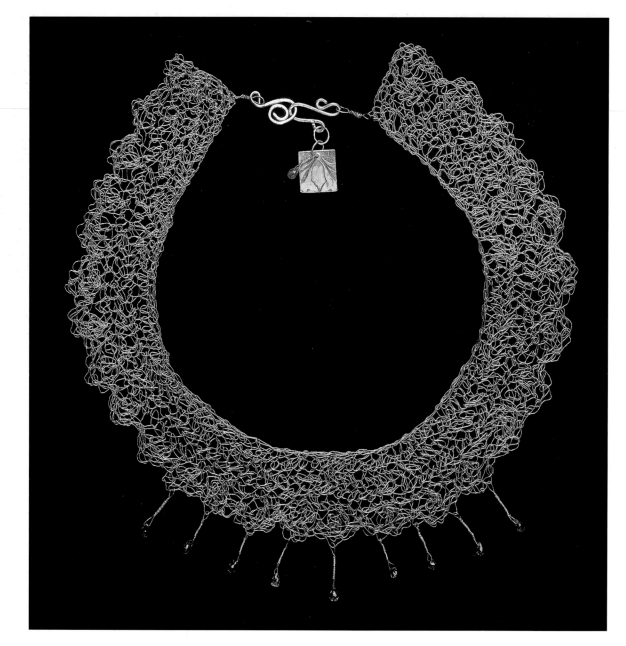

MARIA F. RODRIGUEZ
From the Crocheted Collection:
Brass Collar with Andalusite ■ 2012
21 x 18 x 0.3 cm
28-gauge brass wire, andalusite beads, brass tag;
crocheted, hand formed and hammered, etched
PHOTOGRAPHY BY ANGEL TUCKER

JANNA NOELLE
Porcelain Jasper Trillion Necklace ■ 2012
25 x 15 cm
Custom-cut porcelain jasper, sterling silver, freshwater
pearls, wire; filigree, framed, bezeling with pierced
detail, granulated, soldered, wire wrapped
PHOTOGRAPHY BY ROBERT DIAMANTE

CAROL BLACKBURN
Conical Bead Necklaces ■ 2012

Each: 66 cm long
Polymer clay, sterling-silver beads
PHOTOGRAPHY BY ARTIST

LESLIE MATTHEWS
Three Times—We Parted—Breath and I ■ 2011
Each: 7 x 8 x 3 cm
Sterling silver, polyurethane resin forms; cast
PHOTOGRAPHY BY GRANT HANCOCK

395

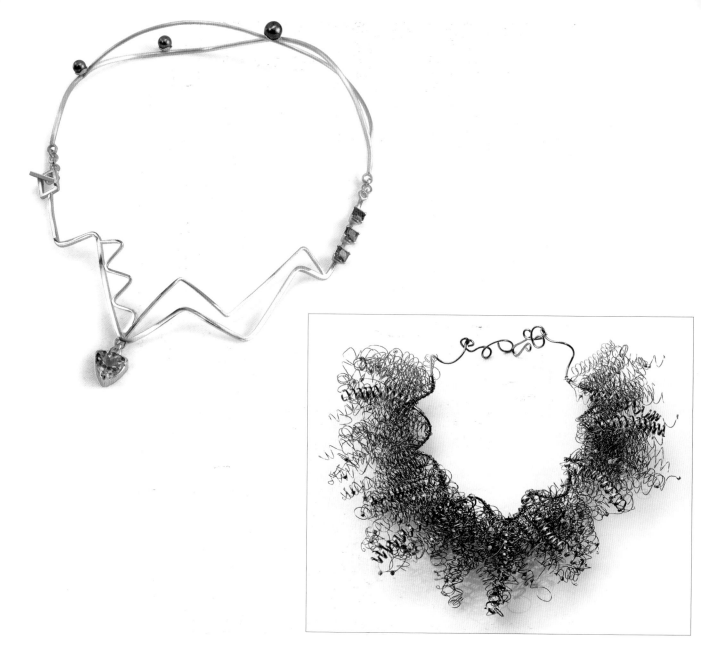

IVANNE BINETRUY
Inclination Necklace ■ 2010

22 x 16 x 3 cm
Sterling silver, blue topaz,
synthetic rubies, pearls
PHOTOGRAPHY BY PAUL AMBTMAN

CARLA BRONZINI
Collana Onde Blue ■ 2011

27 x 25 x 6 cm
Nickel-silver wire, bicone
crystals, turquoise
PHOTOGRAPHY BY ARTIST

Showcase 500
art necklaces

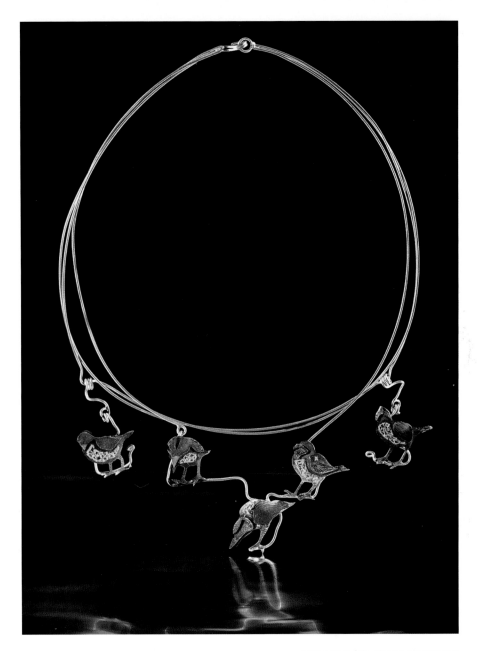

VICTOR SALDARRIAGA TOMIC
Pajaros ■ 2012
20 x 20 x 3 cm
Silver, thread
PHOTOGRAPHY BY LASIERPE

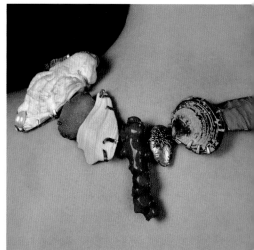

NANCY MEGAN CORWIN
Whidbey Island Water ■ 2010

51 x 15 x 2.5 cm
Argentium sterling silver, seashells, beach
glass, ammonite, coral, sterling silver, pearls
PHOTOGRAPHY BY DOUGLAS YAPLE

KAREN MITCHELL
Fetish ■ 2010

32 x 0.5 x 0.3 cm
22-karat hand-alloyed
and fabricated gold, pink
pearls, freshwater pearls
PHOTOGRAPHY BY ARTIST

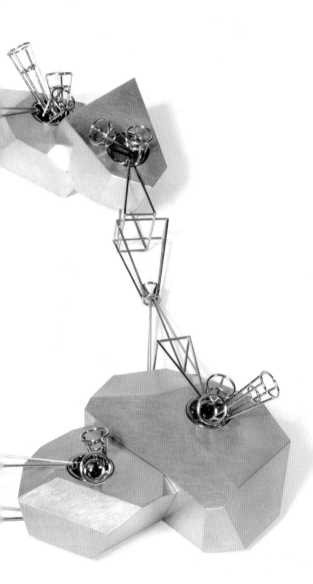

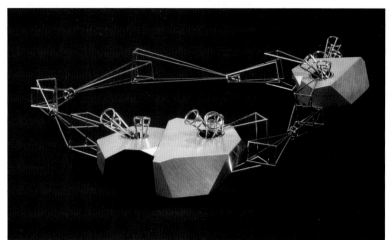

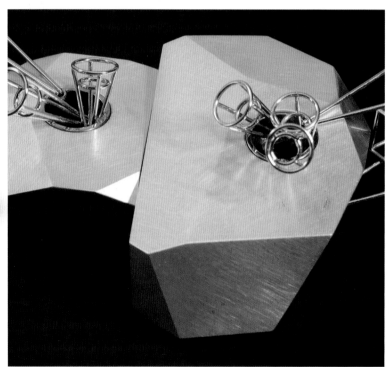

VIVEKA VALENTIN
Meisterstück ■ 2011
18 x 19 x 4 cm
18-karat gold, sterling silver
PHOTOGRAPHY BY ARTIST

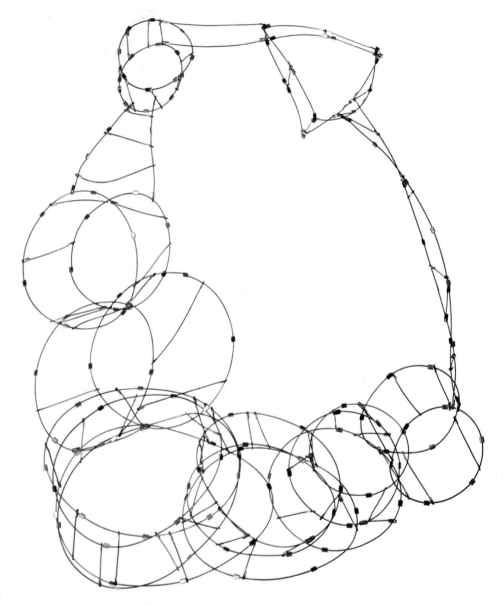

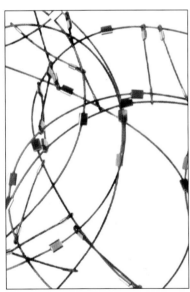

MEGHAN RILEY
Interstitial ■ 2011
35.5 x 20.3 x 7.6 cm
Nylon-coated steel, 14-karat gold fill
PHOTOGRAPHY BY TOKY PHOTOGRAPHY

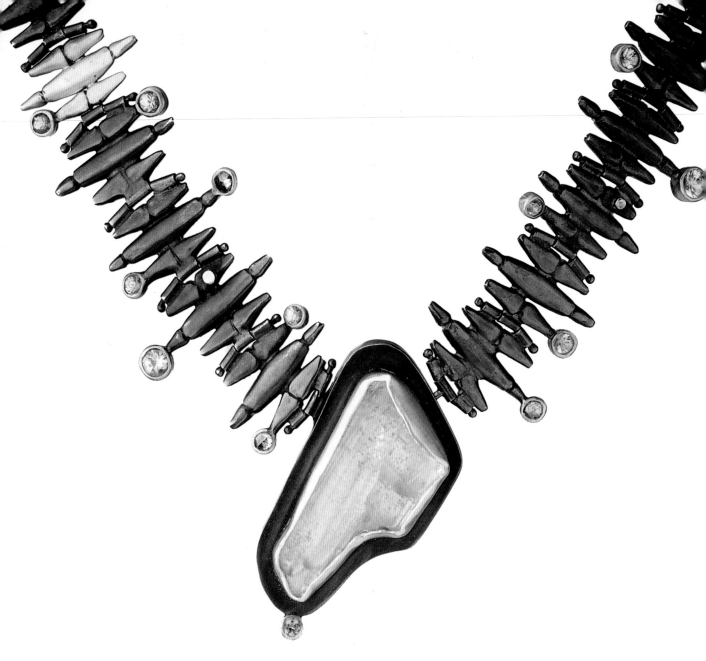

ALISON ANTELMAN
Phenakite Necklace ■ 2012
Overall length: 38 cm
18- and 22-karat yellow gold, sterling silver, blue
zircon, rose-cut diamonds, Nigerian phenakite;
oxidized, hand fabricated and forged, fold formed
PHOTOGRAPHY BY ERIC SMITH

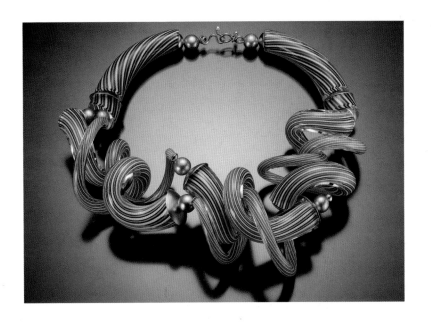

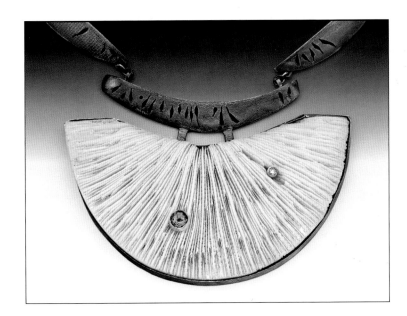

JANINE DECRESENZO
Crescent Coral Necklace ■ 2011

Crescent: 6.5 x 8 x 0.6 cm
Coral, topaz, diamond, sterling
silver; formed, pierced, oxidized
PHOTOGRAPHY BY PETER GROESBECK

JOYCE ROESSLER
Sculptural Necklace ■ 2011

30.4 x 30.4 x 15.2 cm
Glass, sterling silver; fabricated,
hand blown, cut, and shaped
PHOTOGRAPHY BY ROBERT DIAMANTE

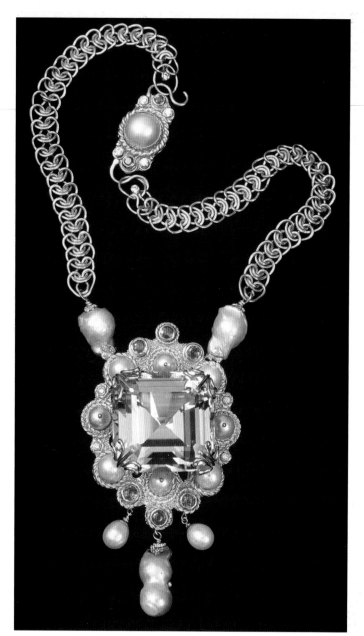

DONNA L. ENGEBRETSON
Rhodes ■ 2010
46 x 9 x 3 cm
22-karat gold, pink kunzite, pink sapphires,
diamonds, baroque South Sea pearls,
freshwater mabe pearl; hand fabricated
PHOTOGRAPHY BY JACK ZILKER

LIAUNG CHUNG YEN
Secret Garden Necklace ■ 2012
21 x 18 x 1.2 cm
22-karat gold, 18-karat gold, black
tourmaline, diamonds; fabricated, set
PHOTOGRAPHY BY HAP SAKWA

405

INGEBORG VANDAMME
Secrets ■ 2010

33 x 33 x 2.5 cm
Anodized aluminum, paper, foam,
thread, ribbon; jewelry-making
and textile techniques
PHOTOGRAPHY BY PETER HOOGEBOOM

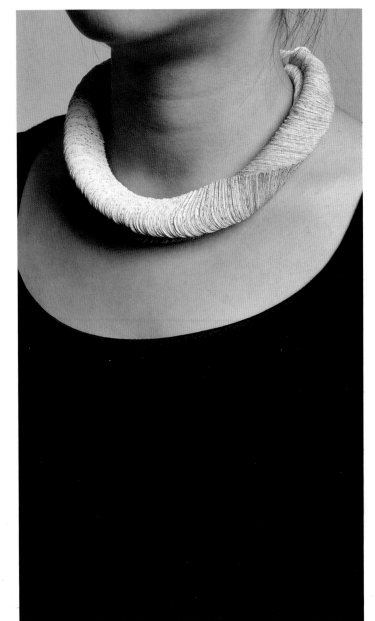

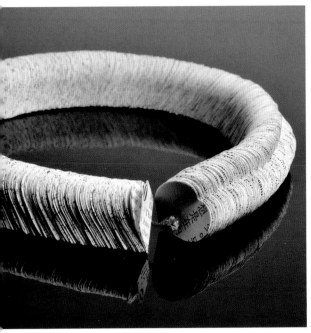

TRICIA TANG
*It Is the Buddhism I Respect and
the Catholicism I Embrace* ■ 2012
16 x 16 x 2.8 cm
The Bible (English version), interpretation of
Prajñāpāramitā Hrdaya Sutra (Chinese version), thread
PHOTOGRAPHY BY EBEE LAM

407

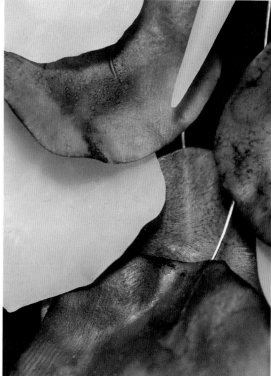

LAURA TABAKMAN
Blue Seeds ■ 2011
Pendant: 4.5 x 3.5 x 0.1 cm
Polymer clay, sterling-silver
wire, steel cable
PHOTOGRAPHY BY ARTIST

FACING PAGE
LOUISE FISCHER COZZI
Back Forth Back Necklace ■ 2012
19 x 38 cm
Polymer clay, oil paint, fine
silver, sterling silver; etched
PHOTOGRAPHY BY GENEVIEVE SAUCIER

Showcase 500
art necklaces

ANDRA O. LUPU
Necklace 1 ■ 2012
20 x 20 x 5 cm
Brass, pigment; hand fabricated
PHOTOGRAPHY BY ARTIST

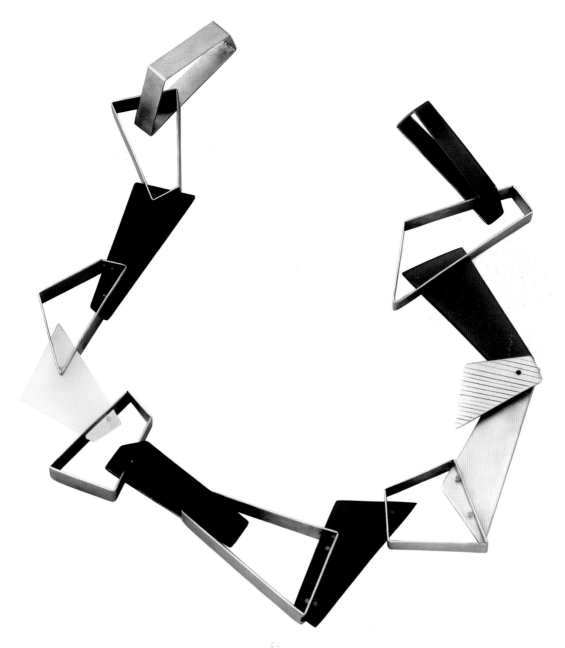

VASIA PACHI
Untitled ■ 2012
50 x 3.5 cm
Silver, acrylic glass
PHOTOGRAPHY BY GEORGE ZARIFIS

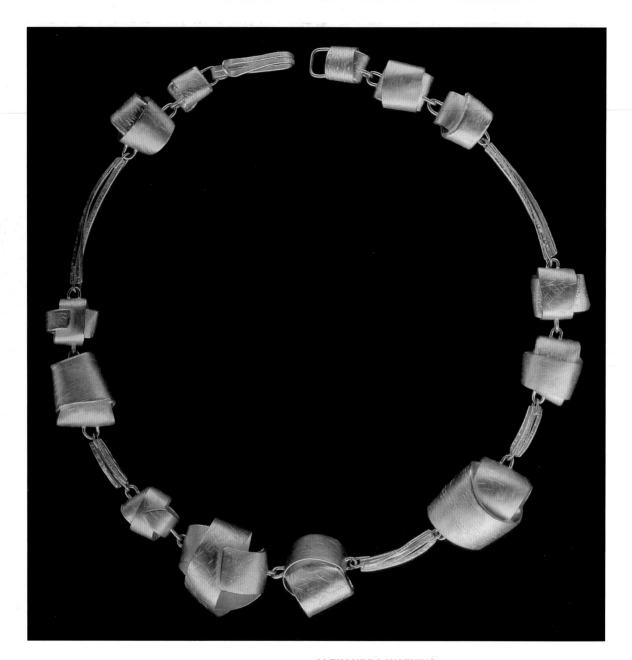

ALEXANDRA WATKINS
Gold Knots ■ 2011

112 x 44 x 3 cm
18-karat gold, 22-karat
gold; hand fabricated
PHOTOGRAPHY BY DEAN POWELL

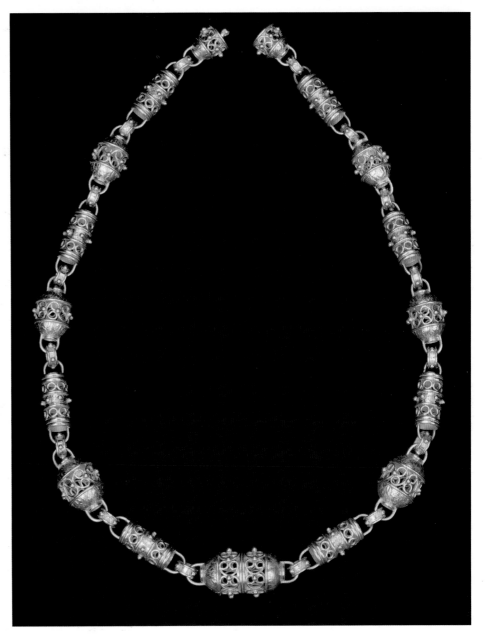

MARY HELLER
Ancient Rhythms II ■ 2011

43.1 x 1.5 x 0.7 cm
22-karat yellow gold, 20-karat yellow
gold, 18-karat yellow gold; hand
fabricated, fused, granulated, soldered
PHOTOGRAPHY BY MARK TRUSZ

413

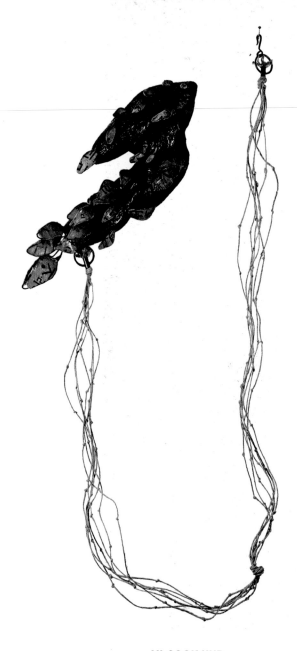

MI-SOOK HUR
Bird Study No. 4 ■ 2012
Overall length: 104 cm
Sterling silver, plastic cast,
steel, paper, hemp string
PHOTOGRAPHY BY ARTIST

DAUVIT ALEXANDER
Supercollider ■ 2012
90 x 14 x 2.5 cm
Silver, corroded iron brake cable, used sewing machine
needles, copper, gold, garnets, natural tourmaline crystals,
chrysoprase, amethyst, diopside, carnelian, citrine, peridot
PHOTOGRAPHY BY ANDREW NEILSON

Showcase 500
art necklaces

LETICIA LLERA
Cleavage ■ 2011
58 x 22 x 1.5 cm
Sterling silver, pearl, shell
button, draft welding tube
PHOTOGRAPHY BY DANNY HERNANDEZ

415

contributors

A

Aalund, Nanz Renton, Washington 378

Abrams, Lauren Jim Thorpe, Pennsylvania 22, 159

Acosta, Luis Utrecht, Netherlands 319

Acosta Contreras, Marian Xalapa, Veracruz, Mexico 147, 344

Agueci, Pilar Verdun, Quebec, Canada 86

Agusti, Alejandra Caba, Buenos Aires, Argentina 295

Ahluwalia, Eina Kolkata, West Bengal, India 13

Albee, Jacob S. Burlington, Vermont 48

Alepedis, Efharis Boston, Massachusetts 345

Alexander, Dauvit Glasgow, Scotland 414

Alexander, Michael New York, New York 339

Antelman, Alison Berkeley, California 402

Arias, Andrea Puerto Ordaz, Bolívar, Venezuela 239

Astratenko, Irina Riga, Latvia 57

B

Bachmann, Karen Brooklyn, New York 217

Bae, Junhee Seoul, South Korea 249

Baird, Kristen Richmond, Virginia 130

Baker, Betsy Charlestown, Massachusetts 338

Bakker, Ralph Rotterdam, Zuid-Holland, Netherlands 377

Banner, Maureen Monterey, Massachusetts 79, 196

Banner, Michael Monterey, Massachusetts 79, 196

Barrett, Dolores Camarillo, California 321

Barthen, Pandora M. Longwood, Florida 12

Bauza, Francisca Krefeld, Germany 340

Beals, Rebecca A. Lubbock, Texas 232

Beaubier, Donald A. Newfoundland, Labrador, Canada 63

Bernard, Michael Dale Milwaukee, Wisconsin 201, 262

Berwanger, Tissa Rio de Janeiro, Brazil 187

Bigazzi, Davide Menlo Park, California 19

Bik, Karolina Mucharz, Malopolska, Poland 267

Binetruy, Ivanne Servon, France 396

Black, Tracy L. San Diego, California 203

Blackburn, Carol London, England 394

Blais, Lauren Jamiaica Plain, Massachusetts 18

Blankenship, Beth Anchorage, Alaska 285

Blessmann, Melanie Edewecht, Niedersachsen, Germany 123

Bodemer, Iris Pforzheim, Baden-Württemberg, Germany 179

Bostwick, Sian Rochester, Kent, England 134

Boudreault, Audrey Coteau-du-Lac, Quebec, Canada 213

Bovè, Jim Washington, Pennsylvania 193

Bowden, Jasmine Exeter, Devon, England 139

Boyd, Leslie D. Brooklyn, New York 290

Brenes, Catalina Empoli, Tuscany, Italy 241

Bronzini, Carla Miami, Florida 396

Brown, Sara Findlay, Ohio 241

Brown, Valerie Fonthill, Ontario, Canada 231

Bucci, Doug Philadelphia, Pennsylvania 136

Buchanan, Ashley Johnson City, Tennessee 222

Buckley, Catherine A. Floral Park, New York 236

Buendia, Lorena N. Distrito Federal, Gustavo A. Madero, Mexico 25

Bugg, Emma L. Hobart, Tasmania, Australia 250

Butterfield, Jenny McMurray, Pennsylvania 149

Byrne, Christiana Houston, Texas 330

C

Cable, Melissa Bellevue, Washington 42

Caid, Kathleen Glendale, California 245

Carricaburu, Kathleen M. Salt Lake City, Utah 162

Castellanos, Anne Buenos Aires, Argentina 115

Chai, Winnie Glens Falls, New York 264

Chang, Alice Bo-Wen Edinburgh, Scotland 135

Cheminee, Matthieu Montreal, Quebec, Canada 11

Cho, Namu Bethesda, Maryland 70, 99

Choi, Jeong-Sun Sungnam-Si, Kyungi-Do, South Korea 91, 121

Choi, Monica North Bergen, New Jersey 93

Christian, Samara M. Sturgeon Bay, Wisconsin 83

Clark, Megan N. Raleigh, North Carolina 265

Clark, Thea Maplewood, New Jersey 173

Class, Petra San Francisco, California 15

Clausen, Jens A. Kautokeino, Finnmark, Norway 235

Cobb, Emily M. Ardmore, Pennsylvania 335

Cobb, Lynn Oakland, California 103

Coderch Valor, Andrea Muro de Alcoy, Alicante, Spain 220

Cohen, Barbara Vancouver, British Columbia, Canada 53

Corwin, Nancy Megan Seattle, Washington 398

Costen, Andrew Vancouver, British Columbia, Canada 230

Cozzi, Louise Fischer Brooklyn, New York 409

Craig, Sally Amherst, Massachusetts 360

Crampton Pipes, Janet Livermore, California 351

Cross, Susan J. Edinburg, Scotland 130

Cullen, Jacqueline L. London, England 229, 249

Culver, Emily Danville, Pennsylvania 332

Czaja, Stephanie Orland Park, Illinois 146

D

Dabiri, Rana Toronto, Ontario, Canada 319

Dam, Annette Copenhagen, Denmark 297

Danch, Laurie Chicago, Illinois 112

Danvers, Gloria St. Augustine, Florida 390

Danylewich, Andrew Liverpool, Nova Scotia, Canada 129

Davis, Renee Palmetto, Florida 231

Davis, Sue Fort Wayne, Indiana 278

De Martino Norante, Margherita Florence, Italy 41

De Syllas, Charlotte Norwich, Norfolk, England 25

Decker, Ute London, England 357

Decresenzo, Janine Philadelphia, Pennsylvania 403

Dees, Hillarey M. Tulsa, Oklahoma 153

Delarue, Marion Carbon-Blanc, France 390

Demmel, Christine Unterschleissheim, Germany 95

Dennis, Diane D. Nokesville, Virginia 242

Desjardins, Josèe Rimouski, Quebec, Canada 175

Dever, Jeffrey L. Laurel, Maryland 316

Di Cono, Margot Lexington, Massachusetts 258

Diebold, Diana M. Houston, Texas 106

Dixon-Ward, Bin Kensington, Victoria, Australia 209

Dizon, Glenn R. San Rafael, California 71

Doge, Noémie Morges, Vaud, Switzerland 49

Donabed, Sandra Jupiter, Florida 269

Donald, Mary Los Angeles, California 184, 324

Dowden-Crockett, Debra Norfolk, Virginia 369

Dusman, Julia New York, New York 371

E

Ebendorf, Robert Greenville, North Carolina 168

Ecuyer, John S. Whangarei, Northland, New Zealand 210

Showcase **500**
art necklaces

Edeiken, Linda San Diego, California 151

Edmonds, Bianca Stratford-upon-Avon, Warkwickshire, England 181

Ellsworth, Wendy Quakertown, Pennsylvania 156

Engebretson, Donna L. Laredo, Texas 404

Errazuriz, Maria G. Santiago, Regiûn Metropolitana, Chile 322

Eversgerd, Emily Telford, Tennessee 155

Evon, Suzanne Weaverville, North Carolina 257

Ewing, Ruann Hindsville, Arkansas 102

F

Fay, Chelsea Rochester, New York 274

Fecker, Jennifer J. Chicago, Illinois 90, 387

Fehlberg-Burns, Kolby Oakland, Colorado 308

Ferguson, Diana Lake Geneva, Wisconsin 309

Ferrero, Tom Windsor, Connecticut 73

Fiala, Anne Indian Head Park, Illinois 67, 260

Field, Margo C. Albuquerque, New Mexico 103

Finelli, Melissa Rockport, Massachusetts 292

Finley, Nancy Aptos, California 314

Fisher, Lindsay Big Rapids, Michigan 312

Fitzgerald, Lilly A. Spencer, Massachusetts 117

Fleming, Kate Rothra Charleston, South Carolina 353

Flouret, Sibylle Marseille, Bouches-du-Rhône, France 382

Ford, Steven Philadelphia, Pennsylvania 338

Forlano, David Philadelphia, Pennsylvania 338

Frazier, Amanda J. Houston, Texas 237

Freller, Elka São Paulo, Brazil 248

G

Gabriel Ribeiro, Nelson Leça Da Palmeira, Matosinhos, Portugal 298

Garcia, Laritza D. Greenville, North Carolina 342

Gaskell, Adrienne Miami, Florida 58, 309

Gaskin, Elliot Seattle, Washington 94, 273

Gassman, Sam Iowa City, Iowa 276

Gerber, Danielle M. Portland, Maine 68

Gilreath, Ashley Gatlinburg, Tennessee 313

Ginnelly, Molly Cowdenbeath, Fife, Scotland 50

Giulietti, David Berkeley, California 10

Glover, Robly A. Lubbock, Texas 247

Gonzalez Mascaro, Dina Vancouver, British Columbia, Canada 219

Griffiths, William Llewellyn Melbourne, Victoria, Australia 182

Grisham, Carole Seattle, Washington 54, 362

Grüner, Tamara Pforzheim, Baden-Württemberg, Germany 111

Guevin, Karina Ange-Gardien, Quebec, Canada 120

H

Hackney, Katy London, England 16

Hall, Lydia T. Altadena, California 383

Hammer White, Wendolyn Rye, New Hampshire 370

Hampel, Christiane Naples, Florida 45

Hanscom, Jennifer Phoenix, Arizona 347

Hashimoto, Liisa Osaka, Japan 143

Hattori, Sumiko Tokyo, Japan 92

Hedman, Hanna L. Stockholm, Sweden 66, 140

Heggland, Liudmyla Rennesøy, Roglaland, Norway 164

Heilman, Bronwen Tucson, Arizona 376

Heinrich, Barbara Pittsford, New York 363

Heller, Mary Toronto, Ontario, Canada 413

Helmond, Mary Ann Kitchener, Ontario, Canada 391

Henry, Rene L. San Diego, California 263

Herb, Heidemarie Perugia, Italy 66

Heuss, Abigail W. Greenville, North Carolina 108

Hill, Joanna Edinburgh, Lothian, Scotland 280

Hiraishi, Yu Tokyo, Japan 240

Hirn, Rosa Pforzheim, Baden-Württemberg, Germany 138

Ho, Janice Hannibal, Missouri 75

Hoogeboom, Peter Amsterdam, Noord-Holland, Netherlands 80

Horine, Susan Mountain Ranch, California 336

Horn, Carole New York, New York 55

Houtman, Maja Utrecht, Utrecht, Netherlands 326

Howard, Aimee M. Lafayette, Louisiana 303

Hu, Jun Beijing, China 133

Huddie, Janet Crownsville, Maryland 143

Hunter, Marianne Rancho Palos Verdes, California 106, 275

Hur, Mi-Sook Greenville, North Carolina 414

Hwang, Jeannie San Francisco, California 100

I

Ichikawa, Kazuhiko Funabashi, Chiba, Japan 256

Ingram, Melissa D. Brisbane, Queensland, Australia 205

Irick, Chris Utica, New York 44

J

Jackson, Debora K. Columbus, Ohio 279

Jestin, Marty Schollang, Germany 191

Jo, Jin Ah Brunswick, Victoria, Australia 199

Johnson, Amy Grand Rapids, Michigan 244

Johnson, Lisa Gatlinburg, Tennessee 331

Jonas, Marty Benicia, California 61, 358

Jordan, BJ Fort Wayne, Indiana 100

Jordan, Greg Fort Wayne, Indiana 100

Juodvalkis, Uosis Prescott, Arizona 88

K

Karash, Deb Bakersville, North Carolina 113

Kariya, Nadine K. Seattle, Washington 142

Kashihara, Erina Machida City, Tokyo, Japan 364

Kaufman, Judith West Hartford, Connecticut 251

Kauhanen, Heli Lahti, Finland 58

Kawai, Satomi Iowa City, Iowa 368

Kemelman, Elida Olivos, Buenos Aires, Argentina 52

Kennedy, Sheridan Sydney, New South Wales, Australia 314

Kerman, Janis Westmount, Quebec, Canada 51

Kim, Hyewon Yongsangu, Seoul, South Korea 266

Kim, Joo Yeon Seoul, South Korea 180, 281

Kim, Junsu Goyang-Si, Gyeonggi-Do, South Korea 310

Kim, Sooyeon Seoul, South Korea 297

Kim, Sooyoung Hopatcong, New Jersey 37

Kim, Sun Kyoung Carbondale, Illinois 192, 288

Kim, Tammy Young Eun San Diego, California 252

Kim, Yong Joo Providence, Rhode Island 152, 188

Kindler-Priest, Linda Bedford, Massachusetts 211

Klakulak, Lisa Asheville, North Carolina 373

Klemm, Susanne Utrecht, Utrecht, Netherlands 122

Knaapi, Sirja Lappeenranta, Finland 35

Kolb, Jocelyn Parkesburg, Pennsylvania 352

Kolodny, Steven Malden Bridge, New York 257

Kortenhorst, Karin Utrecht, Utrecht, Netherlands 26

Krakowski, Yael Vernon, British Columbia, Canada 170

Kramer, Tia Seattle, Washington 63, 342

Kröber, Lisa Tallinn, Estonia 228, 163

Kuebeck, Andrew L. Bloomington, Indiana 189

Kumai, Momoko Kawasaki, Japan 266

Kuo, Chao-Hsien Lahti, Finland 40

Kuo, I-Hsuan Tainan, Taiwan 176

Kuperman, Gal Kfar Uria, Israel 272

Kwon, Jee Hye Brooklyn, New York 127

Kwon, Seulgi Dong-Zack Gu, Seoul, South Korea 74

L

Lakinsmith, Patty Santa Cruz, California 157

Larin, Gregory Bat-Yam, Israel 96

Larson-Voltz, Evan Dearborn, Michigan 197

Lazard, Lorena Mexico City, Mexico 43

Leavitt, Gail Macmillan Palm Beach, Florida 46

Lee, Heng Kaohsiung City, Taiwan 20

Lee, Hyunhee Gyeonggi-Do, South Korea 284

Lee, Iris Toronto, Ontario, Canada 354

Lee, Seung-Hea Providence, Rhode Island 113

Leonard, Laurie Jeannette, Pennsylvania 277

Levier, Kristin D. Moscow, Idaho 64

Liao, Chien Ching Taoyuan, Taiwan 132

Lim, Cesar Beverly Hills, California 158

Lindsay, Richard Santa Fe, New Mexico 84

Lins, Ria E. Mechelen, Belgium 326

Llera, Leticia Mexico City, Mexico 415

Llewellyn, Jenny London, England 60

Lockner, Åsa Stockholm, Sweden 371

Lodge, Jera Cochranton, Pennsylvania 325

Loginova, Anna Toronto, Ontario, Canada 137

Lopez, Edgar A. Santo Domingo, Dominican Republic 243

Lowther, Julia Seattle, Washington 289

Lu, Yenhwa Keelung City, Taiwan 224

Lupu, Andra O. Cluj Napoca, Romania 410

Luro, Maria Buenos Aires, Argentina 72

Lynch, Sydney Lincoln, Nebraska 51

Lyne, Elizabeth A. Cary, North Carolina 228

M

MacDonald, K. Claire Dartmouth, Nova Scotia 117

Machkhas, Ghina Houston, Texas 62

MacKellar, Christine H. Brooklyn, New York 216

MacMullen, W. John Urbana, Illinois 246

MacNeil, Linda Kensington, New Hampshire 271

Mages, Justin Buffalo, New York 91

Maisch, Karin Düsseldorf, Germany 384

Makio, Chihiro Somerville, Massachusetts 30

Makowski, Louise Greenville, Delaware 131

Maksymiuk, Agnieszka Birmingham, England 148

Marcucio, Daniel Portland, Maine 32

Markasky, Evelyn Santa Cruz, California 89, 341

Martin, Jane Bainbridge Island, Washington 165

Maslanka, Vonna L. Deerfield, Illinois 213

Matasick, Sandra J. Gainesville, Florida 107, 140

Matatia, Shirli Haifa, Israel 37

Matthews, Jillian Providence, Rhode Island 227

Matthews, Leslie Adelaide, South Australia, Australia 395

Matych-Hager, Susan Adrian, Michigan 200

Matzakow, Annemarie Freiburg im Breisgau, Baden-Württemberg, Germany 97

McArdle, Claire Newington, Victoria, Australia 145

McCabe, Laura J. Stonington, Connecticut 245

McLaughlin, Barbara Smith Stratham, New Hampshire 207

McMahon, Timothy M. Brooklyn, New York 260

McRuer, Grant R. Dartmouth, Nova Scotia 347

Mendel, Lital Holon, Israel 29

Messam, Lesley Chichester, England 85, 174

Meverden, Becky White Bear Lake, Minnesota 180

Meyns, Sabrina Carrick-on-Shannon, County Leitrim, Ireland 299

Miller, Peggy Melbourne Beach, Florida 322

Miraval, Davinia N. El Paso, Texas 144

Mishly, Iris Kerem Maharal, Israel 329

Mitchell, Ann Tevepaugh Wayland, Massachusetts 55

Mitchell, Karen Aspen, Colorado 399

Mizuno, Chiaki Toyonaka-Shi, Osaka-Fu, Japan 161

Moderhock, Samantha Corinne Glenview, Illinois 163

Montebello, Giancarlo Milano, Italy 215

Moon, Karen Washington, D.C. 365

Morgan, Anne E. Penarth, Wales 291

Morris, Gabrielle N. Belle Mead, New Jersey 255

Morris, Katherine Brooklyn, New York 154

Motuzaite-Kandrataviciene, Simona Ariogala, Raseiniu, Lithuania 385

Muenzker, Viktoria Vienna, Austria 125

Muir, Melanie A. Nairn, Scotland 126

Muir, Thomas P. Perrysburg, Ohio 169

Munsteiner, Tom Stipshausen, Germany 271, 379

N

Nakamura, Satoshi Itami-Shi, Hyogo, Japan 24

Nassif, Kamal L. Providence, Rhode Island 307

Nelson-Smith, Rachel Santa Cruz, California 157

Németh, Krisztina Pápa, Hungary 76

Ni, Xianou London, England 282

Nobe, Satoko New York, New York 166

Noelle, Janna Lake Sherwood, California 393

Nowak Tucci, Kathleen Atmore, Alabama 17, 208

O

O'Harrow, Amber Wellman, Iowa 67, 372

Osgood, Kathryn M. Wanchese, North Carolina 252

Ostenak, Valerie A. Camp Verde, Arizona 323

P

Pachi, Vasia Athens, Greece 411

Pagliai, Mariel Burlington, Ontario, Canada 378

Palomar, Irene Ciudad Autónoma Buenos Aires, Argentina 311

Panzica, Maria Pia La Plata, Buenos Aires, Argentina 160

Papac, Seth San Diego, California 356

Park, Hye Yoon Anyang-Si, South Korea 259

Park, Jeonghye Seoul, South Korea 47, 350

Park, So Young Vestal, New York 85, 361

Pèrez, Marcela Ciudad Autónoma de Bueos Aires, Argentina 359

Perez Demma, Alexandra San Diego, California 42, 356

Petitt-Taylor, Carly A. Knutsford, Cheshire, England 195

Petkus, Aimee Savannah, Georgia 23

Pfrommer, Rahel Stuttgart, Germany 198

Phillips, Carolyn Brazil, Indiana 186

Phillips, Maria Seattle, Washington 189

Podiluk, Mary Lynn Saskatoon, Saskatchewan, Canada 151

Poole, Barbara Charlestown, Massachusetts 208

Poppi, Clare Kenmore, Queensland, Australia 190

Porter, Phoebe Northcote, Victoria, Australia 218

Poterala, Katie L. Greenville, South Carolina 104

Prais-Hintz, Erin L. Stevens Point, Wisconsin 89, 141

Prangley, Sally Seattle, Washington 293

Prins, Katja Amsterdam, Holland, Netherlands 234

Pyle, Judith S. Gettysburg, Pennsylvania 380

Q

Qu, Mengnan Dartmouth, Nova Scotia, Canada 233

R

Ramos, Maria Eugenia Ciudad Autónoma de Buenos Aires, Argentina 77

Rathbun, Heather East York, Ontario, Canada 234

Rauh, Louise Iowa City, Iowa 286

Reed, Todd Boulder, Colorado 36

Renstrom, Judith E. Riegelsville, Pennsylvania 350

Rettich, Linda Bayside, New York 204

Reytan, Denise J. Berlin, Germany 201

Rezac, Suzan Oak Park, Illinois 109, 192

Rice, Jacquelyn Prescott, Arizona 88

Richard, John-Thomas L. Hazel Green, Wisconsin 212

Rickard, Tessa E. Hamtramck, Michigan 334

Riley, Meghan New York, New York 401

Robinson, Mikel Asheville, North Carolina 374

Robson, Lorraine Linlithgow, Scotland 50